JESUS
Among Secular Gods

The Questions of Culture and the Invitation of Christ

RAVI ZACHARIAS
and VINCE VITALE

LifeWay Press®
Nashville, Tennessee

Editorial Team

Vince Vitale
Writer

Reid Patton
Content Editor

David Haney
Production Editor

Jon Rodda
Art Director

Joel Polk
Editorial Team Leader

Brian Daniel
Manager, Short-Term Discipleship

Michael Kelley
Director, Discipleship and Groups Ministry

Published by LifeWay Press® • © 2017 Ravi Zacharias and Vince Vitale • Reprinted October 2018

ISBN 978-1-4627-9327-3 • Item 005801713

Dewey decimal classification: 231
Subject headings: GOD \ JESUS CHRIST—DIVINITY \ GODS AND GODDESSES

"The Apologist's First Question" and "Worship on Empty" taken from *Beyond Opinion* by Ravi Zacharias, Copyright © 2007 by Ravi Zacharias. Used by permission of Thomas Nelson. www.thomasnelson.com

Scripture quotations, unless otherwise indicated, are taken from the Holy Bible, New International Version®, NIV®. Copyright ©1973, 1978, 1984, 2011 by Biblica, Inc.™ Used by permission of Zondervan. All rights reserved worldwide. www.zondervan.com. The "NIV" and "New International Version" are trademarks registered in the United States Patent and Trademark Office by Biblica, Inc.™ Scripture quotations marked NASB are taken from the New American Standard Bible®, Copyright © 1960, 1962, 1963, 1968, 1971, 1972, 1973, 1975, 1977, 1995 by The Lockman Foundation. Used by permission. www.lockman.org. Scripture quotations marked KJV are taken from the Holy Bible, King James Version. Scripture quotations marked ESV are taken from the ESV® Bible (The Holy Bible, English Standard Version®), copyright © 2001 by Crossway, a publishing ministry of Good News Publishers. Used by permission. All rights reserved.

To order additional copies of this resource, write to LifeWay Resources Customer Service; One LifeWay Plaza; Nashville, TN 37234; fax 615-251-5933; call toll free 800-458-2772; order online at LifeWay.com; email orderentry@lifeway.com; or visit the LifeWay Christian Store serving you.

Printed in the United States of America

Groups Ministry Publishing • LifeWay Resources • One LifeWay Plaza • Nashville, TN 37234

Contents

ABOUT THE AUTHORS

RAVI ZACHARIAS is the founder and president of Ravi Zacharias International Ministries (RZIM). For forty-five years Zacharias has spoken all over the world in scores of universities, notably Harvard, Dartmouth, Johns Hopkins, and Cambridge. He has addressed writers of the peace accord in South Africa and military officers at the Lenin Military Academy and the Center for Geopolitical Strategy in Moscow. He has spoken to numerous world leaders and statesmen.

Born in India in 1946, Zacharias immigrated to Canada with his family twenty years later. He received his master of divinity from Trinity International University in Deerfield, Illinois. Well versed in the disciplines of comparative religions, cults, and philosophy, he held the chair of evangelism and contemporary thought at Alliance Theological Seminary for 3½ years. Zacharias has authored or edited more than twenty-five books. Zacharias and his wife, Margie, have three grown children. They reside in Atlanta.

VINCE VITALE is the director of the Zacharias Institute. He was educated at Princeton University and the University of Oxford, and he later taught philosophy of religion as a faculty member at both of these universities. It was during his undergraduate studies in philosophy at Princeton that Vince took an unexpected journey from skeptic to evangelist.

While researching at Oxford, Vince developed a new response to the problem of evil. This response, termed the Non-Identity Defense, is discussed in Vince and Ravi Zacharias's book *Why Suffering? Finding Meaning and Comfort When Life Doesn't Make Sense.* In 2017 Vince and Ravi released a second coauthored book, *Jesus Among Secular Gods: The Countercultural Claims of Christ.*

Vince is married to Jo, who also works with RZIM as the dean of studies for the Zacharias Institute.

INTRODUCTION

Only the truth of Jesus Christ can answer the deepest questions of life. The popular "isms" of today leave the most fundamental questions unanswered. But how can believers learn how to respond to these claims with grace and truth? *Jesus Among Secular Gods* is designed to equip believers to give a reason for the hope they have (see 1 Pet. 3:15).

The rise of secular gods presents the most serious challenge to the absolute claims of Jesus since the founding of Christianity itself. Not only has the Christian worldview been devalued and dismissed by modern culture, but its believers are also openly ridiculed as irrelevant. In this study Ravi Zacharias and Vince Vitale challenge the popular "isms" of the day, skillfully point out the fallacies in their claims and presenting compelling evidence for absolute truth as found in Jesus.

This study will prepare you to face today's most urgent challenges to Christian faith head-on. It will help seekers understand the claims of Christ and will provide Christians with the knowledge to articulate why they believe Jesus stands tall above other gods.

As you complete this study, you will not only learn why Christianity stands tall above secular gods, but you will also be prepared to explain the claims of Christ with gentleness and respect to a world that has embraced these "isms" with fervor.

ACKNOWLEDGMENTS

Many people worked hard to make this project possible, and we are deeply grateful to each of them. Randy Pistor showed enormous skill, insight, and generosity in his work on the personal studies of this project. With her characteristic distinction, Danielle DuRant offered meticulous and discerning comments during the editing phase. My trusted agent, Andrew Wolgemuth, was an eminently wise and attentive guide through the entire publication process. The commitment to excellence of Joel Polk and the entire LifeWay team pointed at every turn and in such an encouraging way to the ultimate excellence of Jesus, who is both the inspiration and the aim of this project.

HOW TO USE THIS STUDY

Jesus Among Secular Gods provides a guided process for individuals and small groups to explore major secular worldviews and examine how followers of Jesus Christ should respond to them. This Bible-study book includes six weeks of content, each divided into three main sections: "Group Study," "Conversational Goal," and "Personal Study." Additional resources are also provided at the back of this book for leaders or individuals who want to study this material in greater depth.

Group Study

Regardless of the day of the week your group meets, each week of content begins with a group session. This group session is designed to last ninety minutes, with approximately twenty minutes devoted to getting started and introducing the week's topic, twenty-five minutes to video teaching, and forty-five minutes to group discussion.

Each group study uses the following format to facilitate simple yet meaningful interaction among group members, with God's Word, and with the video teaching.

Start

This section includes questions to get the conversation started, a review of the previous week's study to reinforce the content, and an introduction to the new content for the current week.

This Week's Topic

This section introduces the new content for the current week.

Watch

This page includes key quotations from the video teaching.

Discuss

This page includes discussion questions that guide the group to respond to the key ideas from the video teaching and to relevant Bible passages. To close this time, you will introduce the week's conversational goal and pray for the conversations you hope to have.

Conversational Goal

Jesus Among Secular Gods presents a great opportunity for individuals to begin gospel conversations with the nonbelievers in their lives. The "Conversational Goal" section provides a simple but engaging question that can be used to begin meaningful conversations about faith with nonbelievers.

Conversational Goal

Here you will find the week's question and a few thoughts to help you begin conversations with people who are not yet Christians.

Journal

A journal page provides space for participants to reflect and process the conversations they have each week with nonbelievers.

Personal Study

Two personal studies are provided each week to take individuals deeper into the ideas that shape secular worldviews and to guide believers to respond to these ideas from a Christian perspective. With biblical teaching and interactive questions, these personal studies challenge individuals to grow in their understanding of God's Word and to make practical application to their lives.

Additional Resources

At the back of this book you will find articles to further develop your understanding of the ideas presented in this study. Twelve articles are provided, two related to each week's study. Additionally, you will find a list of questions designed to start meaningful conversations with people you encounter.

Consider going even deeper into this content by reading the book on which this Bible study is based: *Jesus Among Secular Gods* (FaithWords, 2017).

WEEK 1
Be Prepared

START

Today we have all sorts of information at our fingertips but no idea how to answer the most fundamental and important questions of life. As Ravi said when speaking at Google headquarters, "Just because you have a smartphone doesn't mean you have a wise phone."

We live in an age of choice (when every belief is on our digital doorstep and the endless menu of beliefs can be paralyzing), an age of offense (when choosing one belief over another is branded narrow, exclusive, intolerant, and extremist), and an age of distraction (when teens in America spend nine hours a day using media). These three factors combine to make it more difficult than ever to make an informed decision about the deepest questions of life.

What are some of the biggest questions about life that people regularly ask?

One of those big questions is "What is the meaning of life?" Take two minutes to record a one-sentence answer to this question. Then share your answers with one another.

How do your answers differ from one another? What do they share in common?

9

THIS WEEK'S TOPIC

Use this page to introduce this week's topic.

Our age is one of the most difficult ages in which to be a Christian. A staggering number of students (some have estimated as high as 70 percent) who head to college confessing Christ are no longer active in their faith by the time they graduate.

When it comes to the Christian faith, the cultural landscape has shifted, and the challenges have intensified. It used to be that if you were a Christian, you were thought of as a bit strange, perhaps naïve. Now Christians are often targeted as the enemies of societal progress. More than ever, we need to be prepared to defend a Christian way of seeing the world. But can faith be defended? Many people assume there is a tension between faith and reason.

Richard Dawkins writes:

> *Faith is the great cop-out, the great excuse to evade the need to think and evaluate evidence. Faith is belief in spite of, even perhaps because of, the lack of evidence.*[1]

The biblical definition of *faith,* on the other hand, comes from Hebrews 11:1:

> *Faith is the substance of things hoped for, the evidence of things not seen.*
> **HEBREWS 11:1, KJV**

Which of these two quotations do you think accurately describes faith? Why?

The brilliant seventeenth-century mathematician, physicist, and inventor turned theologian Blaise Pascal claimed that God has given us enough evidence to believe in Him rationally but not so much evidence that we can believe in Him based on reason alone.[2]

Do you think that is a fair statement? Why or why not?
What rational reasons do you have for believing in God?

What elements of your faith go beyond reason?

WATCH

Watch video session 1.

The lordship of Christ is central to the apologist.

RAVI ZACHARIAS

The goal of apologetics is not to vanquish the questioner; it is to win the opponent.

RAVI ZACHARIAS

Sometimes questions come en route to faith.

VINCE VITALE

*Receive all questions as a gift. Asking questions
is the way you get to know a person.*

VINCE VITALE

*Every question is an open door. The answer to any question
is something true, and all truth finds its grounding in God.*

VINCE VITALE

*Don't think of every question as a doubt;
think of every question as a door.*

RAVI ZACHARIAS

*If you give an answer without gentleness and respect, you have cut
off the person's nose, and now you are offering them a rose to smell.*

RAVI ZACHARIAS

The person has to believe you before they believe what you say.

RAVI ZACHARIAS

*A worldview is like a pair of glasses. You're looking
through the lens of certain precommitments.*

RAVI ZACHARIAS

Video sessions available at lifeway.com/jesusamongseculargods
or with a subscription to smallgroup.com

DISCUSS

Use the following questions to discuss the video session.

First Peter 3:15 says:

> In your hearts revere Christ as Lord. Always be prepared to give
> an answer to everyone who asks you to give the reason for the
> hope that you have. But do this with gentleness and respect.
> **1 PETER 3:15**

How many instructions are given in 1 Peter 3:15? (We count five.)
Which of these instructions do you find most challenging? Why?

When people ask hard questions about God and no one takes their questions seriously or provides them with good answers, it is understandable that they come to the conclusion that good answers to their questions must not exist.

Have you ever had a question about faith that you were afraid to ask because you thought people would not respond well?

Have you ever asked a question about faith and felt that you were looked down on for doing so? If comfortable, share about that experience.

Peter encourages us to be ready to ask and answer hard questions. The health of the church in the days ahead, in large part, will be determined by the way we handle questions.

How can we help to make the church a place where challenging questions about faith are welcomed and affirmed?

What are two or three questions about faith you hope you will never be asked by a non-Christian because you would not know how to answer them?

RZIM speaker Michael Ramsden often emphasizes that if you knew the questions in advance for an interview for your dream job, you would spend time preparing to respond well to those questions. The opportunity to remove an obstacle to faith in a person's life is even more important than getting your dream job, so you need to take the time to be prepared.

What can believers do to be personally prepared to respond to questions about faith?

What is one way you hope to be better equipped as a result of this study?

Conversational Goal
Introduce this week's conversational goal.

To put into practice what we are learning, each week we will challenge one another to start conversations about faith with a nonbeliever.

Setting conversational goals in the context of community and encouraging one another in those goals can make an enormous difference in the faithfulness and effectiveness of our attempts to share Christ with others. The goal this week is simply to ask two questions and then to listen well to the answers. These questions are meant to lead you into conversations about faith.

Your conversational goal is to commit during the next week to ask the following two questions of someone who is not yet a Christian.

What is your biggest objection to Christianity?

What do you think it would take for you to change your mind about God and become a Christian?

This week we'll complete the conversational goal, read the articles provided, and complete the two personal studies before the next group session. Next week we'll start by sharing about our conversations and seeing what we can learn from them.

PRAYER
Close your time together with prayer.

Read Ephesians 3:14-21 and make Paul's prayer your own. Ask that God will do immeasurably more than all you ask or imagine, according to His power that is at work within you, through our Bible study together.

CONVERSATIONAL GOAL

Use the following questions to engage with a nonbeliever this week.

During the next week ask someone who is not a Christian:

> ### What is your biggest objection to Christianity?
>
> ### What do you think it would take for you to change your mind about God and become a Christian?

We cannot emphasize enough that when we defend the faith and when we share the faith, we seek to win the person, not just an argument. God didn't come to save questions with clever answers; He came to save questioners through a relationship with Him that is founded on grace. We need to model grace, and that begins by being good questioners and good listeners. As you seek to ask good questions, remember the following words by Ravi.

> *Behind a question is a questioner, and if you do not answer the questioner, you are really not answering the question.*
>
> **RAVI ZACHARIAS**

Here are two reasons we think all questions should be received as gifts.

1. The answer to every legitimate question is something true, and all truth is grounded in God. Therefore, every question, even the most antagonistic one, is an opportunity to share something about who God is and what He has done.

2. For Christians, asking hard questions is not a sign of a lack of faith but an act of worship. When you think about it, asking questions is the way you get to know a person. When you want to get to know people, you ask them deep questions about themselves and listen well to the answers. The same is true of God. God is not a theory. He is personal, and therefore asking deep questions about Him is the way you get to know Him better.

As you seek to have a conversation about faith, remember that listening to the response is as important as asking the question. Listen attentively and sympathetically to the answers you receive. Be ready to respond to their questions, even if you do not have all the answers.

JOURNAL

Use this page to reflect on your conversation with a nonbeliever.

Whom did you speak with? What was your overall experience with this conversation?

_____

_____

_____

_____

_____

How willing was the person to have a conversation with you? What obstacles did you encounter?

_____

_____

_____

_____

_____

What insights did you gain about communicating truth with gentleness and respect?

_____

_____

_____

_____

_____

Personal Study 1
Faith and Reason: Is Faith Blind?

It is Easter Sunday, and in accordance with long-standing tradition, your extended family has gathered at a relative's home for a celebratory meal. Not all of your family members are Christians, but they know that you profess to be one. Even so, relationships have always been amicable.

Entering the living room, you overhear your uncle's conversation in which he makes the following claim: "I've been doing some reading, and while Jesus may have been a decent moral teacher, He certainly wasn't God. All that stuff about His death and resurrection was made up centuries later by corrupt church leaders who were seeking power and money. It's all legend; there's nothing historical about it. That's why they call it faith."

The person with whom your uncle is speaking sees you and, knowing you are a Christian, asks, "Is he right? Is Jesus' resurrection just a legend?"

How would you respond?

Think about your answer to this question as you complete these two studies on being prepared to respond to questions about your faith. You will reflect back on this hypothetical conversation at the end of personal study 2.

The Meaning of Faith

Take a moment to think about the word faith. In a sentence or two, how would you define it?

Compare your definition with the following two definitions.

Faith, being belief that isn't based on evidence, is the principal vice of any religion.[1]
RICHARD DAWKINS

Faith is a response to evidence, not a rejoicing in the absence of evidence.[2]
JOHN LENNOX

How does your definition compare with these two definitions? To which definition is yours most similar?

In what important ways do these definitions differ in their understanding of the relationship between faith and evidence?

Which definition do you often see employed by the world and by the church?

Keep your answers in mind as you continue your study.

The Connection between Faith and Evidence

While it may be surprising, even to some believers, Lennox's definition is actually the true biblical definition of *faith.* The Bible explicitly defines what *faith* means: "Faith is the substance of things hoped for, the evidence of things not seen" (Heb. 11:1, KJV).

Rather than translate the Greek word *elenchos* as *evidence,* newer translations use *assurance* or *conviction.* As a result, the connection between faith and evidence is sometimes overlooked. However, the connection becomes even stronger when we consider that *faith* is a translation of the Greek word *pistis,* which includes the idea of trust.

Putting these pieces together, we see that biblical faith is ultimately belief and active trust in God, based on the spiritual perception of the evidence with which He has provided us. In other words, biblical faith is anything but blind! To quote Lennox once more, "Just as in science, faith, reason, and evidence belong together."[3]

The next time you're engaged in conversation and someone says, "Belief in God is just blind faith," how could you respond?

Recall Bible stories involving biblical heroes, such as Noah, Moses, Joshua, Samuel, David, Peter, or Paul. Look through these stories again, taking note of the specific evidence God provided each of these biblical characters. As you will see, God always provides us with an evidentiary basis for trusting in Him (see 1 John 5:13).

Loving God

In Romans 12:2 the apostle Paul wrote, "Do not conform to the pattern of this world, but be transformed by the renewing of your _____."

Without looking up this verse, what word would you expect to fill in the blank?

Now look up Romans 12:2 in your Bible. What does Paul tell us to renew? Does this surprise you? Why or why not?

The nurturing of the mind is incredibly important for the Christian faith. In fact, it is one way we worship God. When Jesus was asked about the greatest commandment in the law, He replied:

> Love the Lord your God with all your heart and with all your soul and with all your mind and with all your strength.
> **MARK 12:30**

If you have a study Bible, the footnotes for Mark 12:30 cite Deuteronomy 6:5. This key verse in the law commanded the Israelites to:

> Love the Lord your God with all your heart and with all your soul and with all your strength.
> **DEUTERONOMY 6:5**

A visual comparison of these verses reveals something interesting.

Deuteronomy 6:5	Mark 12:30
Heart	*Heart*
Soul	*Soul*
Strength	*Strength*
	Mind

When expounding on the greatest commandment, Jesus added the mind to the list of faculties with which we are to love and worship God. As you reflect on this observation, consider why Jesus did so. (Hint: read 1 Cor. 2:12-16.)

It seems natural to say, "Love God with your heart," for the heart—the seat of our will and desire and emotions—is frequently connected with love in our culture. "I'll love you forever with all my heart" has appeared in many Valentine's Day cards. It also seems natural to say, "Love God with your soul," for the soul is the very essence of our being. But practically speaking, loving God with the mind may be less familiar.

To better understand this concept, read each of the following verses from Proverbs.

Let the wise listen and add to their learning,
and let the discerning get guidance.
PROVERBS 1:5

Instruct the wise and they will be wiser still;
teach the righteous and they will add to their learning.
PROVERBS 9:9

The wise store up knowledge,
but the mouth of a fool invites ruin.
PROVERBS 10:14

How does gaining wisdom allow us to love God with our minds?

What are some ways we could put these calls to cultivate wisdom into practice today?

On a scale of 1 to 10, 1 being not at all and 10 being all the time, how well are you loving God with your mind? Mark a number on the scale.

1   2   3   4   5   6   7   8   9   10

How does loving God with our minds prepare us to give a reason for our Christian faith?

What is one step you will take to love God with your mind this week?

Personal Study 2
A Reasoned Defense

Reclaiming Argumentation

The word *argument* has a bad reputation these days, especially among many Christians. Raise the possibility of providing an argument for the Christian faith, and someone may quote the apostle Paul:

> The Lord's servant must not be quarrelsome but must be kind to everyone.
> **2 TIMOTHY 2:24**

This view is unfortunate because an argument need not be emotional at all. In other words, quarreling and arguing are two very different things. Properly defined, an argument is "a coherent series of reasons, statements, or facts intended to support or establish a point of view."[1] The classic example of a logical argument comes from introductory philosophy courses:

> **PREMISE 1: All men are mortal.**
> **PREMISE 2: Socrates is a man.**
> **CONCLUSION: Therefore, Socrates is mortal.**

This is a sound logical argument. Admittedly, its subject matter is not very interesting, but that is precisely the point. Arguments are not controversial; arguments are true or false, inaccurate or plausible. Rather, it is the subject matter of arguments that can sometimes generate more heat than light.

We all make arguments every day, whether dealing with customers ("This is why your shipment didn't arrive on time") or children ("Too much sugar will make you sick") or spouses ("We need to follow our budget"). With arguments it is the delivery or the intent—often to illustrate why another person is mistaken—that triggers an emotional response. For this reason arguments must be presented graciously and respectfully, as Peter urged: "Do this with gentleness and respect" (1 Pet. 3:15). However, nothing is emotional or improper about an argument itself.

God and Argumentation

In the context of evangelism, a natural objection arises from all this: "You cannot argue someone into the kingdom of God." And to a fair extent this is indeed true.

Scripture is very clear that new birth, eternal life, forgiveness of sins, and adoption into God's family are acts of God, not humans. Through the process of conversion, a person goes from spiritual death to spiritual life. No human argument is capable of such a feat; this is a supernatural act of God. Even so, argumentation is important in helping to remove intellectual barriers to faith in Christ.

Read the following passages and reflect on ways God approved of using argumentation to thoughtfully engage with others.

Job 38:1–42:6: What approach did God take in dealing with Job? How did Job respond?

Isaiah 1:18-20: When speaking to the Israelites and urging them to repent, what is suggested by God's invitation to "reason together" with Him (v. 18, ESV)?

2 Corinthians 10:5: What is the significance of Paul's claim that "we demolish arguments" and "take captive every thought to make it obedient to Christ"?

The Early Church

Argumentation is just one approach the first disciples used to engage with their Jewish, Greek, Samaritan, Roman, Ethiopian, and other non-Christian neighbors.

Read each verse and circle the action verbs that describe the early believers' approach to contending for the gospel.

With many other words he warned them; and he pleaded with them, "Save yourselves from this corrupt generation."

ACTS 2:40

23

*Day after day, in the temple courts and from house to house, they never
stopped teaching and proclaiming the good news that Jesus is the Messiah.*

ACTS 5:42

[Saul] talked and debated with the Hellenistic Jews, but they tried to kill him.

ACTS 9:29

*The Berean Jews were of more noble character than those in Thessalonica,
for they received the message with great eagerness and examined
the Scriptures every day to see if what Paul said was true.*

ACTS 17:11

*[Paul] witnessed to them from morning till evening, explaining
about the kingdom of God, and from the Law of Moses and
from the Prophets he tried to persuade them about Jesus.*

ACTS 28:23

What stands out to you in this list?

How do these Scriptures challenge your view of evangelism?

**Why might evangelism include more than sharing a simple version
of the gospel?**

Historical Truth, Not Legend

Not only did the early church value the importance of thoughtfully engaging with
others on matters of truth, but it also placed a premium on faithfully preserving and
transmitting important evidence about Christ. The clearest example of this effort
is known as a creed, which is a concise formula of religious belief. In other words,
a creed consists of important truths compressed into as few words as possible.
Brevity made creeds easy to memorize, retain, and pass along from one generation
to the next, which was important for both teaching young Christians and being
prepared to defend the faith from intellectual attack.

The New Testament incorporates in its pages ancient creeds that already existed prior to its composition. One of the most important creeds is recorded by the apostle Paul in 1 Corinthians 15:

> *What I received I passed on to you as of first importance: that Christ died for our sins according to the Scriptures, that he was buried, that he was raised on the third day according to the Scriptures, and that he appeared to Cephas, and then to the Twelve. After that, he appeared to more than five hundred of the brothers and sisters at the same time, most of whom are still living, though some have fallen asleep. Then he appeared to James, then to all the apostles, and last of all he appeared to me also, as to one abnormally born.*
>
> **1 CORINTHIANS 15:3-8**

New Testament scholars have identified a number of different factors indicating that this passage is actually a creed of the early church. Which begs the question, When did Paul learn the creed? Certainly, he must have learned it prior to his visit to Corinth (see Acts 18:1); otherwise, he could not have taught it to the Corinthians. The most likely explanation is that Paul learned the creed from Peter and James during his visit to Jerusalem three years after his conversion (see Gal. 1:18-19). When recounting his time there, Paul used the Greek term *historeo*, which means "to gain a historical account,"[2] to describe his visit with Peter (see v. 18). Because many scholars date Paul's conversion between AD 31 and AD 33,[3] the creed would therefore be quite early.

It can safely be concluded that the resurrection of Jesus is not a legendary development. Legends and myths take several generations to develop. Because the creed recorded in 1 Corinthians 15:3-8 was formulated at most just a few years after Jesus' crucifixion, there was no possible way for legendary elements to creep in. The window of time between the events themselves and the creed's formulation was far too small for such corruption to occur. What Paul reported to the Corinthians therefore reflects the beliefs of the very first Christians. The historical foundations of the Christian faith are indeed firm.

Based on this week's personal studies, how could you respond to your uncle, who asserted that Jesus' resurrection is a legend that developed over time (p. 16)?

For further study read the articles on pages 124–27.

WEEK 2
Atheism and Scientism

START

*Use the following content to begin group session 2.
Start by discussing last week's conversational goal.*

For our first conversational goal we asked someone who is not yet a Christian two questions.

> What is your biggest objection to Christianity?

> What do you think it would take
> for you to change your mind about
> God and become a Christian?

Was the person willing to talk? Did you enjoy the conversation?

What were the most common objections?

What underlying experiences or concerns motivated each of these objections?

What did people say it would take for them to accept Christ?

Sometimes objections are linked to negative experiences that people have had. Sometimes objections are linked to concerns about fairness or justice, for people to be treated lovingly, or for beliefs to be based on evidence. Sometimes even more important than finding the flaws in objections to faith is finding underlying points of agreement that can be starting points for further conversation.

As we hope to share Christ with those who do not know Him, we are not interested in winning debates just for the sake of it. We are interested in lovingly introducing people to the person of Jesus Christ and to what He has done for them.

27

THIS WEEK'S TOPIC

Use this page to introduce this week's topic.

I love sports. But here is a sporting experience I would never want to have. Imagine being thrown into a game without knowing when it started, when it will finish, what the objective of the game is, or what the rules are. What would you do? You would probably ask the other players around you to answer those four questions for you.

What if they responded with many different answers? Or what if they simply carried on playing, uninterested in your questions and looking at you oddly for asking them? Next you would look to a coach for help, but what if the coach was standing there looking at the chaos and yelling, "Great job, guys! You're all doing great! Keep going! We've got a first-place trophy waiting for all of you!"

Now imagine the conversations about the game on the drive home. They would be completely meaningless. It is our knowledge of the start, the finish, the objective, and the rules of a game that provides us with the freedom to play it and enjoy it in a meaningful way.

Sadly, this is not just a game; this is a reality for many who are struggling to live a meaningful life in our culture. As a society, we are losing the answers to these four crucial questions.

1. ORIGIN: *Where did I come from?*
2. MEANING: *Why am I here?*
3. MORALITY: *How should I live?*
4. DESTINY: *Where am I going?*

Your answers to those four fundamental questions form the basis of your worldview—the lens through which you experience and interpret the world around you, which therefore influences the way you choose to live.

We all need answers to the deepest questions of life. Our aim in *Jesus Among Secular Gods* is to put Christianity alongside the other major ways of seeing the world, in a respectful way, so that people can make an informed decision about what to believe and how to live.

Do you think Christianity or atheism does a better job of answering the four questions of origin, meaning, morality, and destiny? Why?

The number of Americans who identify as atheists has roughly doubled in recent years. Why do you think that is the case?

WATCH
Watch video session 2.

ATHEISM: *the idea that there is no God*
SCIENTISM: *the idea that science explains everything*

Criticism without alternative is empty.
VINCE VITALE

The atheist worldview critiques without offering any alternative.
VINCE VITALE

With God I can answer numerous questions. Without God most fundamental questions are unanswerable.
RAVI ZACHARIAS

Science is not only compatible with the existence of God, but it actually points to the existence of God.
VINCE VITALE

Not only does science not disprove God; only God proves science.
VINCE VITALE

When you talk about evil, you assume there's good. When you assume there's good, you assume there's a moral law to differentiate between good and evil. And if you assume a moral law, you must assume a moral lawgiver. If there is no moral lawgiver, there is no moral law. If there is no moral law, there is no good. If there is no good, there is no evil.
RAVI ZACHARIAS

You cannot assume intrinsic worth for personhood unless there is a personal, moral First Cause for creation.
RAVI ZACHARIAS

Video sessions available at lifeway.com/jesusamongseculargods
or with a subscription to smallgroup.com

DISCUSS

Use the following questions to discuss the video session.

The video session suggests that atheism and scientism have trouble explaining reality.

> **What fundamental questions of life do atheism and scientism leave unanswered?**

> **Do you think it takes more faith to be a Christian or to be an atheist? Why?**

An atheist might say, "I don't need to defend anything, because I'm not claiming to believe anything. I'm simply claiming not to believe in God. Therefore, the burden of proof is not on me but on the person who believes in God." Richard Dawkins puts it this way:

> *If you want to believe in ... unicorns, or tooth fairies, Thor or Yahweh—the onus is on you to say why you believe in it. The onus is not on the rest of us to say why we do not.*[1]

> **Do you agree with this statement by Dawkins? Why or why not?**

> **How do atheism and scientism subtly creep into the Christian life?**

Many people have heard unfounded rumors that science has disproved God, and without thinking it through, they have jumped from science to scientism—from the welcome fact that science can explain a lot to the deeply problematic assumption that it can explain everything. Quite to the contrary, science actually points to God.

> **Someone who holds to scientism might say, "We used to need God to explain rain and rainbows and shooting stars, but now we have scientific explanations of these things, so we no longer need God." How would you respond?**

> **Read Psalm 19:1-2. How does the Bible answer the claims of scientism?**

Vince referred to philosopher Immanuel Kant, who said two things fill the mind with awe: "the starry heavens above me and the moral law within me."[2] Here Kant echoes the Bible's affirmation that God's attributes "have been clearly perceived, ever since the creation of the world, in the things that have been made" (Rom. 1:20, ESV) and that God's law "is written on [people's] hearts, while their conscience also bears witness" (Rom. 2:15, ESV). Science and morality point to God.

While many believe that science has disproved God, in fact only God proves science:

> *When you talk about evil, you assume there's good, when you assume good, you assume there is a moral law by which we differentiate between good and evil, and if you assume a moral law you must assume a moral lawgiver. If there's no moral lawgiver, there's no moral law, if there's no moral law, there's no good, if there's no good, there's no evil.*
>
> **RAVI ZACHARIAS**

Based on Ravi's statement, when someone raises a moral objection to God, what question could you ask to help show the tension underlying their objection?

Conversational Goal

Introduce this week's conversational goal.

During the next week ask someone who is not a Christian:

> Have you ever had an experience in your life
> that made you think there might be a God?

Feel free to ask the same person you conversed with in week 1 or select a different person. It may take the person a minute to respond to such a deep question, so let them know you are not in a rush and give them time to reflect.

PRAYER

Close your time together with prayer.

Read Psalm 8 together and reflect on the progression it shows from wonder at God's creation to an appreciation of God's grace and finally to a response of worship. Consider reading the psalm aloud as a group, taking turns as each member reads one verse.

CONVERSATIONAL GOAL

Use the following question to engage with a nonbeliever this week.

This week's conversational goal is particularly exciting because it introduces a question that has the potential to lead to many deep, life-changing conversations about the Christian faith.

During the next week ask someone who is not a Christian:

Have you ever had an experience in your life that made you think there might be a God?

Feel free to ask the same person you conversed with in week 1 or select a different person. It may take the person a minute to respond to such a deep question, so let them know you are not in a rush and give them time to reflect.

After you have listened well to the person's initial response, possible follow-up questions could include the following.

Why did that experience make you think there might be a God?

Have you had any other experiences that made you think there might be a God?

How does the idea of the existence of a God make you feel?

Would you like for God to exist? Why or why not?

Remember to pray about your conversation in advance. As you seek to start conversations, always remember that God is sovereign over all your interactions. These talks are divine appointments, both for you and the person with whom you are speaking.

JOURNAL

Use this page to reflect on your conversation with a nonbeliever.

Whom did you speak with? What was your overall experience with this conversation?

_____

_____

_____

_____

_____

How willing was the person to have a conversation with you? What obstacles did you encounter?

_____

_____

_____

_____

_____

What insights did you gain about communicating truth with gentleness and respect?

_____

_____

_____

_____

_____

Personal Study 1
Science and God

Imagine you are going out to coffee with a friend, and in the course of conversation he says to you, "There's just no scientific evidence for God's existence. That's why I'm an atheist. Science is the way we study the world around us, and it's been remarkably successful at discovering new things and improving human technology and lives. Good scientists don't believe in God; otherwise, they couldn't do their work. Religious belief is unscientific, so why should I believe in God?" Your friend's comments reveal as much about his definition of *science* as they do about his disbelief in God.

> *How would you respond?*

Think about these claims as you complete these two studies on atheism and scientism. You will revisit this conversation at the end of personal study 2.

Defining Science

> *How would you define the word* science *in a sentence or two?*

> *What are some assumptions you have about science's ability to explain the world?*

Consider the following definitions of *science*.

[Science] by definition deals only with the natural, the repeatable, that which is governed by law.[1]	*The essence of true science is a willingness to follow empirical evidence, wherever it leads.*[2]
MICHAEL RUSE	**JOHN LENNOX**

How does your definition compare with these two definitions? To which definition is yours most similar?

What stands out to you in these two definitions? Which definition is broader, and which is narrower? Which definition has the immediate effect of excluding God from the realm of science?

The Compatibility of God and Science

John Lennox also writes:

> *Contrary to popular impression, there is no one agreed scientific method, though certain elements crop up regularly in attempts to describe what "scientific" activity involves. … But precise definition is very elusive.*[3]

Michael Ruse's proposed definition reflects a modern trend of smuggling a commitment to atheism into the definition of *science*. Ruse insists that science "by definition deals only with the natural," but this statement itself is philosophical, not scientific. Yet history reveals that there is no conflict between God and science. The vast majority of prominent scientists throughout history were theists; most of them, in fact, were Christians. Rather than being a hindrance to their science, their belief in God was a major inspiration for it.[4]

For example, Johannes Kepler (1571–1630), who formulated the laws of planetary motion, described his motivation "to discover the rational order which has been imposed on [the universe] by God, and which he revealed to us in the language of mathematics."[5] Therefore, any assertion that God and science are in conflict or are incompatible should be recognized for the misleading claim that it is. Of the scientists who responded to a 1996 survey conducted by the journal *Nature*, approximately 40 percent indicated that they believed both in a God who answers prayer and in personal immortality.[6]

What does Kepler's example suggest to you about the possibility of being a Christian who believes in both God and the value of science? Has this ever been a point of tension for you?

How does science enhance your belief in God?

Why is it unhelpful and unnecessary to think about God and science in mutually exclusive terms?

The General Created Order Points to God

The Bible has much to say about the inferences we should draw from observing the world around us. With science freed from its unnecessary naturalist baggage, let's now heed Lennox's advice "to follow empirical evidence, wherever it leads." That evidence reveals five features of the created order that present a significant problem for atheism but are readily explained by the biblical worldview.

FEATURE 1
The universe had a beginning.

THE ISSUE
Science and philosophy affirm that the universe had a beginning, but can atheism account for the change from nothing to something?

As recent scientific and philosophical evidence affirms, the universe had a beginning and has not existed eternally, contrary to Aristotle's view that dominated scientific thinking for centuries.[7] In other words, the available academic evidence reveals that everything—matter, energy, space, and time—came into existence *ex nihilo,* or "out of nothing."

Science and philosophy do not supply all the evidence. Read the following passages.

In the beginning God created the heavens and the earth.

GENESIS 1:1

The heavens declare the glory of God;
the skies proclaim the work of his hands.

PSALM 19:1

By faith we understand that the universe was formed at God's command,
so that what is seen was not made out of what was visible.

HEBREWS 11:3

According to these Scriptures, what does the natural world reveal about God as Creator?

Ultimately, science and philosophy have merely confirmed what the Bible has unambiguously affirmed for centuries. Robert Jastrow, a former NASA astronomer, humorously summarizes the point:

For the scientist who has lived by his faith in the power of reason, the story ends like a bad dream. He has scaled the mountains of ignorance; he is about to conquer the highest peak; as he pulls himself over the final rock, he is greeted by a band of theologians who have been sitting there for centuries.[8]

Atheism has no answer for the creation of something from nothing. Within the materialistic confines of the atheistic worldview, the universe is all there is, and it cannot create itself. God possesses the necessary attributes to create a universe such as ours.

- God is immaterial: "God is spirit" (John 4:24).
- God is eternal: "Stand up and praise the LORD your God, who is from everlasting to everlasting" (Neh. 9:5).
- God is all-powerful: "I am the LORD, the God of all mankind. Is anything too hard for me?" (Jer. 32:27).

Atheism cannot account for the change from nothing to something, but Christianity can. Things do not just pop into existence for no reason. If the universe began to exist, there should be an explanation for its existence. The best explanation is that the cause of the universe is something highly powerful and highly creative from outside space, and it is hard to think of a better candidate for that description than God.

How does reflecting on God's character and attributes lead us to appreciate the way the world has been made?

Why is God the best and most plausible explanation for the beginning of the universe?

FEATURE 2
The universe is finely tuned for life.

THE ISSUE
Can atheists explain the fine-tuning of the universe by random chance?

To say the universe is finely tuned for life means that a universe as complex as ours meets all the conditions necessary to sustain life. As even atheists like Sir Fred Hoyle and Christopher Hitchens have admitted, the fine-tuning argument is a compelling argument against atheism. The fact that the universe is so finely tuned for life, to such a precise degree that it defies comprehension, cries out for explanation. And a compelling explanation is exactly what the Bible provides.

Atheism can explain the amazing fine-tuning of our universe only by appealing either to (1) random chance with a probability of success essentially equal to zero or to (2) an unsubstantiated metaphysical guess such as the multiverse (the idea that our universe is just one of many). However, the Bible offers a much more plausible explanation for the reason our universe is so perfectly suited for life (see Job 38:33; Ps. 19:1; 136:5; Isa. 45:18; Heb. 11:3). Our universe is not the product of random chance; there is an ultimate object or aim to our universe. In His love and wisdom, God established the laws of the heavens by creating, fashioning, commanding, and ordering our universe so that we could inhabit it.

How do God's intentionality and purpose complement, rather than contradict, the evidence from science about the fine-tuning of the universe?

How could the order and function we see in the world around us provide a way for you to begin a conversation about God with an unbeliever?

Personal Study 2
God's Fingerprints

For this study we pick up where the first study left off.

FEATURE 3
The universe is regular.

THE ISSUE
How do we explain that the universe has carried on with regularity,
and why do we assume that it will continue to do so in the future?

Observing the world, we find that the universe is regular. That the universe should operate in a regular manner, with absolute predictability day after day, seems like the most obvious of observations. But if we can get past our familiarity and look at the situation with fresh eyes, we will realize that the uniformity of nature is utterly surprising and requires a good explanation. Why should the universe be regular rather than irregular or wildly irregular?

What regular, observable patterns have you seen in the world around you?

What conclusions about the world can you make on the basis
of these observations?

Ultimately, scientists accept the uniformity of nature as a matter of faith. As physicist Paul Davies comments:

> *Just because the sun has risen every day of your life, there is no guarantee that it will rise tomorrow. The belief that it will—that there are indeed dependable regularities of nature—is an act of faith, but one which is indispensable to the progress of science.*[1]

For a Christian, this act of faith is a reasonable one, for it is based on the character of God, who cares for us and wants us to live orderly and coherent lives in which we can find meaning. Consider the following verses, which describe the way God maintains the regularity of the universe.

He is before all things, and in him all things hold together.
COLOSSIANS 1:17

The Son is the radiance of God's glory and the exact representation of his being, sustaining all things by his powerful word.
HEBREWS 1:3

Absent a being like God, who sustains creation at all moments and in whom all things hold together, atheists have no explanation for why the universe has always operated with such regularity and will continue doing so. From a naturalistic viewpoint it is a great mystery. God alone provides the explanatory resources to adequately account for this feature of the universe that we inherently take for granted.

Why is a regular universe necessary for us to live orderly and coherent lives in which we can find meaning?

FEATURE 4
The universe is knowable.

THE ISSUE
Atheistic evolution aims at survival, not truth, so why assume that our beliefs are in any way reliable?

Albert Einstein remarked:

The most incomprehensible thing about the universe is that it is comprehensible. ... One should expect a chaotic world, which cannot be grasped by the mind in any way.[2]

It is remarkable not only that the universe is comprehensible but also that we have minds to comprehend it. Because atheistic evolution is not aimed at truth—how we behave in order to survive is all that matters, not what we believe—atheists have no explanation for this feature of existence.

To an atheist, the success humans have experienced in discovering and comprehending the universe is utterly surprising if our reasoning and cognitive faculties have developed (that is, evolved) in a manner that prioritizes only beliefs that aid survival and reproduction, regardless of whether such beliefs are true. In contrast, the comprehensibility of the universe and the ability of human minds to explore its workings are entirely consistent with the picture of humanity set forth in the Bible.

The Bible is absolutely clear that humanity is a miraculous, special act of creation rather than the result of a blind, unguided evolutionary process. In particular, the Bible affirms three important truths about each of us.

1. We are each made in the image of God (see Gen. 1:26-27; 2:7; 5:1-2). God is a rational being, and therefore we are rational beings as well. This means we have every reason (absent extenuating circumstances) to trust our minds to guide us to what is true.
2. Each of us is "fearfully and wonderfully made" (Ps. 139:14). We are created beings, not cosmic accidents.
3. "We are God's handiwork" (Eph. 2:10). Each of us was created for a purpose, and therefore God has imbued our lives with dignity and meaning.

Of the three truths listed above, which most often leads you to praise God? Why?

Additionally, the Bible suggests that rather than reveal all knowledge to us in advance, God chose to leave the discovery to us because He delights in our exploration of the universe. Like a loving parent, God is pleased by our wonder and amazement that result from exploring His creation:

> *Great are the works of the LORD;*
> * they are pondered by all who delight in them.*
> **PSALM 111:2**

> *It is the glory of God to conceal a matter;*
> * to search out a matter is the glory of kings.*
> **PROVERBS 25:2**

Unlike with atheism, we can trust our minds because God takes delight in seeing us use our minds to understand His creation.

How does the existence of our minds and our ability to discover constitute evidence against atheism and in favor of theism?

FEATURE 5
The universe is moral.

THE ISSUE
How can someone ground morality in something other than God?

Recall the inscription on Kant's tombstone: "The starry heavens above me and the moral law within me." There seems to be a moral law within each of us. While any number of factors—culture, sin, drugs, abuse, or mental illness—can alter or suppress our moral reasoning, the ability to engage in meaningful moral reasoning appears innate. Consider these examples.

- C. S. Lewis remarked that his "argument against God was that the universe seemed so cruel and unjust. But how had I got this idea of just and unjust? What was I comparing this universe with when I called it unjust?"[3]
- America's founding document, the Declaration of Independence, makes one of the most profound moral statements in all of human history: "We hold these truths to be self-evident, that all men are created equal, that they are endowed by their Creator with certain unalienable Rights, that among these are Life, Liberty and the pursuit of Happiness."
- The Universal Declaration of Human Rights, which was adopted by the United Nations General Assembly in 1948, declares in article 1 that "all human beings are born free and equal in dignity and rights. They are endowed with reason and conscience and should act towards one another in a spirit of brotherhood."[4]

How closely does the vision of morality presented in these statements align what you read in the Bible?

Consider your nonbelieving friends. On what do they base their idea of right and wrong?

Our governments, our laws, and our inner conscience declare that we are moral beings. But what accounts for this fact? According to atheistic thinkers Michael Ruse and Richard Dawkins, morality is an arbitrary and, worse still, illusory evolutionary by-product. And yet we persist in making moral pronouncements or, in the case of immoral behavior, moral denouncements. Moreover, when we do so, we believe that our words are both real and meaningful.

The Bible explains why this is so. Consider the following two verses, which address morality and the human heart.

> *[Gentiles] show that the requirements of the law are written on their hearts, their consciences also bearing witness, and their thoughts sometimes accusing them and at other times even defending them.*
> **ROMANS 2:15**

> *The heart is deceitful above all things and beyond cure. Who can understand it?*
> **JEREMIAH 17:9**

Each verse reveals an important truth. First, morality is not grounded in human reason. Rather, we use reason to discern the moral law that God has written on our hearts. Second, no amount of secular human reasoning will take us to morality, for the human heart is warped by sin and beyond the ability of any human (but not God) to repair.

Some atheists, such as Sam Harris in his book *The Moral Landscape,* certainly attempt to bypass these conclusions, using science. But science cannot answer the deep moral questions of life. There are two clear reasons for this reality.

1. Using science to answer moral questions is a category mistake. As John Lennox remarks:

> *Science can tell you that, if you add strychnine to someone's drink, it will kill them. But science cannot tell you whether it is morally right or wrong to put strychnine into your grandmother's tea so that you can get your hands on her property.[5]*

2. A moral law requires a moral lawgiver:

> *An impersonal force won't do because a moral rule encompasses both a proposition and a command; both are features of minds.*[6]

The moral notions of justice, love, and mercy make sense only when communicated from one person to another; such notions are devoid of meaning when divorced from personhood. And to account for the ubiquitous nature of moral obligation, we must posit a personal God whose character provides an absolute standard of goodness.

The moral law is therefore ultimately grounded in the person of God and derives from His character. As God told the Israelites, "Be holy because I, the LORD your God, am holy" (Lev. 19:2).

If there are limits to what scientific data can tell us about reality and if "the things that come from the Spirit of God" are "discerned only through the Spirit" (1 Cor. 2:14), what are the risks of utilizing a scientific approach in all aspects of our walk with God?

Why is it important to leave room for the spiritual as well as for observations based on science?

Equipped with this information, how could you respond to your friend at the coffee shop (p. 34) who asserted that science and belief in God are incompatible?

In what ways do you need to adjust your own thinking about science and belief of God?

For further study read the articles on pages 128–32.

WEEK 3
Pluralism

START

Use the following content to begin group session 3. Start by discussing last week's conversational goal.

We hope in the past week you had the chance to ask someone:

> Have you ever had an experience in your life that made you think there might be a God?

How did the person respond?

What can we learn from the answers we received?

What would you do differently if you had the same conversation again?

Would you ask that question again?

How could you revise, adapt, or add to this question if you ask it again?

THIS WEEK'S TOPIC

Use this page to introduce this week's topic.

"All views are equally valid." This is the form of pluralism we will discuss this week. It claims that although our opinions about the deep questions of life may seem different on the surface, they are actually fundamentally the same or at least of equal merit. This might seem like an affirming, generous position to hold, but there are problems with it.

The logical problems with this view surface almost immediately. Does the view that all views are equally valid also apply to the view that all views are not equally valid? RZIM speaker Abdu Murray had a conversation with a student who said he did not think it was his place to disagree with anyone. Abdu responded, "Sure you do." The student replied, "No, I don't." Abdu said, "You just did."

Vince had a related conversation at Portland State University. A student said to him, "I think there's a universal human longing for peace, and I think it points to the reality of something that can fulfill that longing, the way hunger points to the reality of food." So far Vince was following him. But then the student concluded, "So I think it's a good idea to believe in something, whatever that is." He had an assumption that all big-picture worldviews would meet this universal human need more or less equally well.

What secular gods do people worship? Why don't those gods bring peace? What would have to be true of a worldview to provide ultimate peace?

As we have previously discussed, as important as it is for us to find flaws in mistaken worldviews, it is often even more important to find points of agreement that can act as starting points for conversation and relationship. Despite its logical problems, many people are attracted to pluralism.

What are some good and honest motivations that lead to belief in pluralism? Why are people attracted to it?

A friend was considering enrolling his kids in a reading program. He asked, "What are they reading?" The leader of the program responded, "Anything, just as long as they are reading." It is interesting that we would never respond that way about eating. We would never think it is OK to eat anything, just as long as we are eating.

Why do you think, as a society, we are happy to judge right and wrong when it comes to what we put in our bodies but are averse to judging right and wrong with respect to what we put in our minds and souls?

WATCH
Watch video session 3.

> **PLURALISM:** *all views are equally valid.*

*Two mutually exclusive statements both cannot
be true at the same time and in the same sense.*
RAVI ZACHARIAS

You have to have a point of reference for absolute thinking.
RAVI ZACHARIAS

*We're afraid of truth because truth leads to disagreement,
and we don't know how to disagree anymore.*
VINCE VITALE

*Jesus disagreed with us. His very coming was an act of disagreement
with us, an act of saying that our lives had disagreed so badly
with what He intended for us that we required saving.*
VINCE VITALE

In Christianity we have a God who is both love and truth.
VINCE VITALE

Love without truth is not love. Truth without love is not truth.
VINCE VITALE

*The West is flirting with total chaos unless language returns
to meaning and moral values return to absolutes.*
RAVI ZACHARIAS

Religions are fundamentally different and only superficially similar.
RAVI ZACHARIAS

DISCUSS

Use the following questions to discuss the video session.

The Perceived Trajectory of Truth

In the video Ravi and Vince talked about the nature of disagreement. When you are faced with disagreement, is your instinct to fight or flee? In what ways?

What are the positive and negative aspects of your reaction?

Where do you see examples in our culture of love at the expense of truth or truth at the expense of love?

$$\frac{\begin{array}{l} God = Love \\ God = Truth \end{array}}{Truth = Love}$$

Jesus on the cross is simultaneously the greatest act of God's disagreement with us and the greatest act of God's love for us. Only in Jesus does truth equal love, and therefore only Jesus can get us out of the cultural ultimatum we are stuck in: fight or flee. Every other worldview makes a choice between love and truth. Jesus refused to, because in Him and only in Him, love and truth are one and the same.

What are concrete examples of holding love and truth together in unity that you have experienced or heard about?

As Christians, what would it look like for us to express our disagreement with others in our very act of sacrificial love for them, as Jesus did for us?

One misconception that can lead to pluralism is the assumption that, at the end of the day, most of the major worldviews are pretty much the same. On the contrary, Ravi argues that the world's major worldviews are fundamentally different and at best superficially similar.

If someone asked you to identify three key unique features of Christianity, what would you share?

How has Christianity made a practical difference in your life? How does this difference demonstrate the uniqueness of Christianity?

Conversational Goal

Introduce this week's conversational goal.

During the next week ask someone who is not a Christian:

If God exists, what do you think He thinks of you?

This question can often expose that the God someone is rejecting is not the God of the Christian faith. Some people may respond by saying they think God would be indifferent toward them. Other people may respond by talking about what God would think of the way they have recently behaved. Be aware that there may be truth in this second response, but the question is not about what God thinks of your behavior but, more specifically, what God thinks of you.

PRAYER

Close your time together with prayer.

Read Isaiah 40:25-26 and allow these verses to guide your prayer. Let's come before God in prayer, confessing times when we have put our trust or found our identity in anyone or anything other than Him and declaring that He is our one and only God and Savior.

CONVERSATIONAL GOAL

Use the following question to engage with a nonbeliever this week.

Perhaps the greatest uniqueness of the Christian faith is God's unconditional love for every person. Often this is one of the most challenging Christian beliefs for people to accept, because many people—both Christians and non-Christians— struggle to believe that they are lovable and that they are loved.

During the next week ask someone who is not a Christian:

If God exists, what do you think He thinks of you?

This question can often expose that the God someone is rejecting is not the God of the Christian faith. Some people may respond by saying they think God would be indifferent toward them. Other people may respond by talking about what God would think of the way they have recently behaved. There may be truth in this second response, but the question is not about what God thinks of your behavior but, more specifically, what God thinks of *you*.

This conversation can provide an opportunity to share with people that although God may be pleased or displeased with various aspects of their behavior, one primary answer to this question is that God loves them, He thinks of them as His beloved creation, and He longs to be in relationship with them. This may be a new, exciting idea to people who have previously thought of God more like Santa Claus—someone who keeps a list of their naughty and nice deeds so that He can either reward or punish them, who stops by only once a year, and who never stays long enough to say hello.

In our broken world of disappointments and shattered dreams, what a gift it is to be able to share with people that they are deeply loved. The story in Luke 15 of the prodigal son, who did everything wrong but who was still extravagantly loved by his father and invited back into relationship with him, may be a powerful story to share with anyone who does not know about God's universal, unconditional love.

JOURNAL

Use this page to reflect on your conversation with a nonbeliever.

Whom did you speak with? What was your overall experience with this conversation?

_____

_____

_____

_____

_____

How willing was the person to have a conversation with you? What obstacles did you encounter?

_____

_____

_____

_____

_____

What insights did you gain about communicating truth with gentleness and respect?

_____

_____

_____

_____

_____

Personal Study 1
The Exclusivity of Truth

Imagine you are having dinner with a friend who expresses the following pluralistic response to Christianity. Looking up from dinner, he says, "Christianity just seems— I don't know—somehow arrogant. I mean, think about it. When Christians assert that their beliefs are true and that Jesus is the only way to God, they're claiming that everyone else is wrong. They're effectively saying that everyone who disagrees with them and doesn't accept Jesus is condemned to hell. Doesn't that strike you as rather narrow-minded? How can Christians be so right and everyone else so wrong? Where's the humility in that?"

How would you respond?

Think about these claims as you complete these two studies on pluralism. You will revisit this dinner conversation at the end of personal study 2.

E Pluribus Unum

The traditional motto of the United States is the Latin expression *e pluribus unum*— "out of many, one." In many cases plurality is a desirable thing. At its best, America's society is a wonderful human tapestry woven together from the lives of millions of people with different languages, music, food, literature, art, and ethnicities. We celebrate the ideal of diversity, even though it is imperfectly realized, by engraving it on the nation's seal and coinage. It is indeed a worthy aspiration, one that has inspired many noble causes.

Furthermore, diversity is an ideal that God values. Consider the way the apostle John described his supernatural vision of heaven:

After this I looked, and there before me was a great multitude that no one could count, from every nation, tribe, people and language, standing before the throne and before the Lamb. They were wearing white robes and were holding palm branches in their hands.

REVELATION 7:9

According to God's own revelation, every "nation, tribe, people and language" will be represented in heaven. Heaven will be the place where those "out of many" who have placed their trust in Jesus Christ will come together to worship the One. The ethnicity of each person is sacred because ethnicity is an essential, immutable component of personhood, and each person is made in God's image. Thus, it is no surprise that heaven, the place where God will dwell with His people forever (see Rev. 21:3), reflects the diversity of His image bearers.

In what ways does Christianity embrace diversity?

If every "nation, tribe, people and language" will be represented in heaven, how should diversity affect our understanding of the Great Commission (see Matt. 28:18-20; Acts 1:8)?

Disagreeing without Being Disagreeable

People, however, are not the same as beliefs. It is incredibly important not to confuse the reality of a pluralistic society (that is, a society that includes people of diverse beliefs) with being a pluralist about truth. The former is desirable because all people are equally valuable; the latter is incoherent and should be rejected.

Consider the following. Although all people are equally valuable, the same cannot be said for their beliefs. Unlike people, who are intrinsically valuable because they bear the image of God, beliefs are merely true or false. What makes a belief valuable or valid is whether it is true. In other words, beliefs that are true and undergirded by strong evidentiary support are preferable to those that are false and lacking in evidence.

In your own words, describe the difference between being pluralistic in culture and being pluralistic in truth.

Certainly, it is tempting to want to affirm all beliefs as equally valid in order to be inclusive and avoid the risk of offending friends, family members, or work colleagues. This fear is understandable; no one wants to be viewed as narrow-minded, arrogant, dogmatic, or bigoted. But affirming all beliefs as equally valid results in two mistakes.

1. It confuses a person with his or her beliefs. Criticizing a belief, if done respectfully, is not the same as criticizing the person who holds that belief.
2. Affirming all beliefs as equally valuable is, for all practical purposes, equivalent to claiming that all ideas are equally right, equally correct, or equally true.

While Christians should always heed biblical admonitions to disagree without being disagreeable (see Col. 4:6; 1 Pet. 3:15), they are called to disagree at times when false ideas are being passed off as true.

> **Read the following passages and consider the instructions Paul supplied early church leaders for correcting error and adhering to truth.**

> *Watch your life and doctrine closely. Persevere in them,*
> *because if you do, you will save both yourself and your hearers.*
> **1 TIMOTHY 4:16**

> *The time will come when people will not put up with sound doctrine.*
> *Instead, to suit their own desires, they will gather around them a great*
> *number of teachers to say what their itching ears want to hear.*
> **2 TIMOTHY 4:3**

> *He must hold firmly to the trustworthy message as it has been taught, so that*
> *he can encourage others by sound doctrine and refute those who oppose it.*
> **TITUS 1:9**

> **What are some ways we could put these commands into practice today?**

What is the most difficult aspect of holding to these truths in the manner Paul described?

As these verses demonstrate, Paul clearly thought some beliefs were more valuable than others because they were true, and "knowledge of the truth … leads to godliness" (Titus 1:1). Therefore, Paul urged his readers to correct, rebuke, warn, and exhort others and to respond to unsound teaching and false doctrine with the truth. But he also encouraged them to do so "with great patience and careful instruction" (2 Tim. 4:2) because God's servants must be "kind to everyone" and "not resentful" (2 Tim. 2:24). Paul was teaching his young leaders the important skill of disagreeing without being disagreeable.

What is the difference between disagreeing and being disagreeable?

Who do you know who models disagreement well? What could you learn from their example?

Jesus Is the Truth

Why this emphasis on valuing truth? Because the same God who values the plurality of human diversity flatly rejects the notion of pluralism about truth itself. In Scripture we see this fact in two primary ways.

1. Jesus asserted that He is "the way and the truth and the life" (John 14:6). Notice that Jesus did not just claim to be someone who speaks or teaches the truth; He claimed to be truth itself—truth incarnated in human form (see Phil. 2:5-11). Therefore, everything Jesus said and did is true and authoritative.
2. Jesus followed up this statement with another: "No one comes to the Father except through me" (John 14:6). The early church was not ambiguous on this point. Consider the following statements by Jesus and His apostles.
   - Jesus: "This is eternal life: that they know you, the only true God, and Jesus Christ, whom you have sent" (John 17:3).
   - Peter: "Salvation is found in no one else, for there is no other name under heaven given to mankind by which we must be saved" (Acts 4:12).
   - John: "Whoever has the Son has life; whoever does not have the Son of God does not have life" (1 John 5:12).
   - Paul: "There is one God and one mediator between God and mankind, the man Christ Jesus" (1 Tim. 2:5).

Therefore, despite all the options in the marketplace of religions, not all paths lead to God (or claim to). Eternal life and salvation—intimate, loving relationship with God—are found in Christ alone and no one else (see Rev. 3:20).

Admittedly, the exclusivity of such a claim rubs many people the wrong way. However, truth by its very definition is exclusive, because asserting that something is true involves an implicit assertion that its negation is false. In other words, what is true must logically exclude its opposite. As Ravi has explained:

> The gospel of Jesus Christ is beautiful and true, yet oftentimes one will ask, "How can it be true that there is only one way?" Odd, isn't it, that we don't ask the same questions of the laws of nature or of any assertion that lays claim to truth. We are discomfited by the fact that truth, by definition, is exclusive. That is what truth claims are at their core. To make an assertion is to deny its opposite.[1]

Even though the exclusivity of Jesus' claims can upset other people, why should we still share them, even if theses truths are unpopular?

If the statements of Jesus, Peter, Paul, and John are all true, then as a matter of reality, no other person, including Mohammed, Buddha, Confucius, or oneself, can provide eternal life or salvation other than Jesus Christ. Moreover, these statements are quite reasonable because they are truth claims, and there is nothing extraordinary about the exclusivity of a truth claim. What matters in the end is whether such truth claims are in fact true and how we really know they are true. We will turn to that discussion in the second part of this week's study.

The human heart is wired in such a way that even if God provided 1,000,000 ways to reach Him, we would complain that 1,000,001 are not available to us. What is the relationship between our sinful hearts and our denial of truth?

Why should the exclusivity of Jesus delight and not dismay us?

Before you came to Christ, what if any of the truth claims of Christianity were difficult for you to reconcile? How did you ultimately reconcile them and turn to Christ in faith?

Personal Study 2
Christianity and the Tests for Truth

Knowing Truth

As Ravi has explained in many of his talks over the years, there are three tests for truth that a worldview must satisfy in order to be credible.

1. A worldview must be logically consistent, meaning its teachings cannot be self-contradictory. This first test is critical because it excludes worldviews that are ultimately incoherent or systemically contradictory.
2. A worldview must be empirically adequate. In other words, its teachings must match what we see in reality. Without this criterion we may end up believing a logically consistent fairy tale.
3. A worldview must be existentially relevant. A worldview's teachings must speak directly to questions of meaning and the way we actually live our lives; otherwise, we have only an academic theory and not an effective way of viewing the world.

Thus, we can think of these three tests for truth as a sort of worldview filter. Unfortunately, screening each worldview using this filter would greatly exceed the scope of this study. However, it is instructive to use these tests for truth to compare Christianity with the underlying motivations of pluralism.

The Motivations of Pluralism

Three good, God-given desires commonly motivate pluralism.

1. *Equal value.* Pluralism can be motivated by a commitment to the equal value of every person.
2. *Equal opportunity.* Pluralism can be motivated by fairness. People should have equal access to the truth or equal opportunity to discover the truth.
3. *Equal unity.* Pluralism can be motivated by a longing for unity and community.

However, pluralism applied to religious truth is ultimately flawed. While these legitimate motivations find only a partial and distorted fulfillment in pluralism, they are completely fulfilled by Christ in a manner that satisfies all three tests for truth. Let's consider each motivation individually.

MOTIVATION 1: EQUAL VALUE. One reason people turn to pluralism is the good desire that all people should be valued. However, in Christianity all people have inherent worth and value. All people are loved by God, not just the people who have chosen to follow Him.

> *Read the following Scriptures and record what they teach about God's love for you.*
>
> *Matthew 10:29-31*
>
>
> *John 3:16*
>
>
> *Romans 8:38-39*

As our colleague Abdu Murray explains, God's love, Jesus' sacrifice, and our inherent value are inseparably bound together:

> *The incarnation and the cross are profound demonstrations of the value we have in God's eyes and of our inherent dignity. They tell us that our actions are significant because they have consequences. And they tell us that God must address those consequences, but in a way that saves us from ourselves— because he values us. ... At the cross God paid an infinite price to show our infinite value. As a triune being, he does not need relationship with us to have relationship. He has it within himself in the eternal community of the Trinity.[1]*

God's love is the one and only thing that is equal for every person. As the apostle Paul made clear, God's love never changes and cannot be lost. In the end human value is personal and measured by the value-conferring love of a personal God "who did not spare his own Son, but gave him up for us all" (Rom. 8:32).

The Christian narrative about God's love and our value satisfies the tests for truth. Because God is a triune being, Jesus the Son could pay the penalty for our sin by dying on the cross. The divine transaction of substitutionary atonement between the Son and the Father was very real and not a sham. Moreover, the events of Jesus' death and resurrection can be verified through historical inquiry.

Finally, Jesus is existentially unique among the founders of major world religions. Jesus offers us rest from our troubles; He bears our burdens; He comes to us and rescues us; He provides salvation as a free gift; and unlike the founder of every other belief system, He lovingly takes our guilt on Himself. Jesus journeys through life with us, sustaining us along the way.

How does God's love for us in Christ make Christianity distinct from other belief systems?

MOTIVATION 2: EQUAL OPPORTUNITY. A second admirable motivation for pluralism is a desire for all people to have access to the truth, yet God has already provided this opportunity to all people.

Read the following Scriptures.

You will seek me and find me when you seek me with all your heart.
JEREMIAH 29:13

Yet to all who did receive him, to those who believed in his name, he gave the right to become children of God.
JOHN 1:12

Here I am! I stand at the door and knock. If anyone hears my voice and opens the door, I will come in and eat with that person, and they with me.
REVELATION 3:20

What do these Scriptures teach about God's desire to know people in a personal relationship?

As professor Clay Jones of Biola University notes, the gospel has spread throughout much of the world:

> More people attended Christian services in China last Sunday than attended Christian services in all of Western Europe combined. …
> At Pentecost, Parthians, Medes, Elamites, Mesopotamians, Egyptians, Libyans, Romans, Asians, "both Jews and proselytes, Cretans and Arabians" heard the gospel (Acts 2:9-11). Tradition has it that the apostle Thomas brought Christianity to India in AD 52. There are Christian tombstones in China dated no later than AD 86. The Ethiopians consider the Ethiopian eunuch mentioned in [Acts 8:26-39] to be the founder of Christianity in their country. Paul personally brought the gospel to Greece, what is now Turkey, and then to Rome, which was the center of the civilized world in his day.[2]

We certainly do not know everything about the ways God reveals Himself. However, we can be sure of this: all who want Him will find Him.

Though Christianity is often accused of being too narrow, why is it actually more open than pluralism?

Have you ever believed Christianity to be to narrow? Why? What made you think this way?

God's standards for entering the kingdom are eminently fair. As pastor Andy Stanley asks:

> *What could be fairer than this? Everybody is welcome. Everybody*
> *gets in the same way. Everybody can meet the requirement.*[3]

In other words, Jesus' starting point is everyone else's finish line—the assurance of salvation (see John 5:24; Rom. 10:9; 1 John 5:13).

Here the claims of Christianity once again pass the tests for truth. There is nothing logically inconsistent with God's promise to reveal Himself to those who seek Him, for it is God Himself who planted eternity in the hearts of people. As Augustine said:

> *You have made us for yourself, O Lord, and our hearts*
> *are restless until they find their rest in you.*[4]

We see this reality confirmed by the manner in which God has made the gospel known throughout the centuries to various people groups all over the world. Finally, through the presence of God, who is always near, the deepest longings of our hearts are satisfied.

MOTIVATION 3: EQUAL UNITY. A final motivation for pluralism is a longing for unity with other people. Yet we see that God's purpose for us is to be in community as He has been in eternal community with the Persons of the Trinity: Father, Son, and Holy Spirit. From eternity past God has existed in community.

As Christians, we discover a unity of diversity in the community of the Trinity. As theologian William G. T. Shedd explains:

> *God is not a unit, but a unity. ... God is blessed only as he is self-knowing*
> *and self-communing. A subject without an object could not experience either*
> *love or joy. Love and joy are social. They imply more than a single person.*[5]

Thus, the three trinitarian Persons love one another (see John 3:35), dwell in one another (see John 14:10-11), know one another (see Matt. 11:27), address one another (see Heb. 1:8), glorify one another (see John 17:5), confer with one another (see Gen. 1:26; 11:7), plan with one another (see Isa. 9:6), send one another (see John 14:26), and reward one another (see Phil. 2:5-11; Heb. 2:9). God is very much a being in relationship!

While the concept of a triune being exceeds our full comprehension, there is nothing contradictory in asserting that God is one being (one *what*) and three Persons (three *whos),* for personhood and essence are separate categories. And while the Trinity is disclosed only by special revelation from God rather than by natural theology, Jesus' revelation as the Son of God is confirmed by His resurrection from the dead (see Acts 17:31). Finally, it makes sense that we too would hunger for unity and community, for these things characterize the God whose image we bear. The community we long for reflects the perfect eternal community of the Trinity, and communion with God awaits us in heaven (see Rev. 21:3).

Pluralism has become a pervasive worldview, but for questions of theological truth, why is it important to remember that we are aliens and strangers in this world (see Rom. 12:1-2; 1 Pet. 2:11)?

When have you been guilty of treating different worldviews as if they are equally valid? In what ways has pluralism crept into the way you evaluate the world?

Having completed this week's personal studies, how would you respond differently to your pluralistic friend (p. 54)?

For further study read the articles on pages 133–38.

WEEK 4
Humanism and Relativism

START

Use the following content to begin group session 4. Start by discussing last week's conversational goal.

What did people say in response to the question:

> If God exists, what do you think He thinks of you?

How did your conversation proceed from there?

What do these conversations tell us about the ways people view God?

What do these conversations tell us about the ways people view themselves?

Would you ask this question again if you had the opportunity?

If so, how might you adapt it or add to it?

THIS WEEK'S TOPIC

Use this page to introduce this week's topic.

Relativism is a word that is thrown around a lot. While relativism takes a variety of forms, the basic idea is that truth is not the same for all of us. We are told to pursue our own truth and to be true to ourselves. We are told that all truth is relative to the individual, and therefore maybe Jesus is true for you but not for me.

But there is a clear problem with saying, "All truth is relative." Does that include the truth that all truth is relative? Is that truth also relative? If so, then what reason do I have to believe you when you tell me that all truth is relative? Maybe even that truth is true for you but not for me.

Here is another way to see the problem with relativism. Say someone asks you a question and you give an answer, and then the other person says, "That's not true." If you can always say, "Well, it's true for me even if not for you," that would lead to the complete breakdown of conversation and therefore the complete breakdown of relationship.

Relativism about morality is particularly frightening and particularly devastating for society. How can we trust one another when a grave evil committed against you or your family can be justified with the words "It may have been evil for you, but it was good for me."

Relativism naturally leads to humanism, which means that human beings are the ultimate measure of truth. Relativism claims that we can create our own truth, morality, and meaning on an individual level. Humanism, at least in its atheistic form, claims that humanity can create its own value, meaning, and purpose on a societal level. It is up to humanity to save itself.

Have you come across examples of relativism or humanism in conversations you have had? What examples come to mind?

What are some examples of relativistic or humanistic influence on today's culture?

If humanism becomes the dominant worldview, what impact do you think that will have on the future of society?

WATCH
Watch video session 4.

> **RELATIVISM:** *all truth is relative.*
> **HUMANISM**: *we can make progress on our own.*

*If we do away with objective truth, what's left
to make decisions about what to believe?*
VINCE VITALE

You cannot live just in this world and still find meaning.
RAVI ZACHARIAS

*Relativism is the handmaid of humanism because man becomes
the measure of all things. But nobody tells you which man.*
RAVI ZACHARIAS

Part of humanism is a mantra of progress.
VINCE VITALE

*Where do you get human value and human potential
if you take God out of the picture?*
VINCE VITALE

*The funeral at which real life begins for each of us
is the burying of one's own pride and self-sufficiency.*
RAVI ZACHARIAS

*When you see your heart as God sees your heart,
you see what He has provided for you in the cross.*
RAVI ZACHARIAS

The decision of every human heart: self-reliance or God-reliance
VINCE VITALE

Video sessions available at lifeway.com/jesusamongseculargods
or with a subscription to smallgroup.com

DISCUSS

Use the following questions to discuss the video session.

Secular humanism believes we can look to human advancement for justice, peace, and the end of suffering. Humanism is guided by the idea of progress.

Do you think we are making progress as a society? Why or why not?

Early humanists were Christians motivated by their belief that God had bestowed value on human beings, but today's atheistic humanism holds to an elevated sense of human value and ethics while rejecting God. A serious problem emerges with this approach. Any plausible ethical theory acknowledges the equal value of every person. But for every person to be equally valuable, there has to be something that is equally true of every person.

If God did not exist, can you think of anything that would be equally true of every person?

How does being made in the image of God imbue all people with inherent and equal value?

Humanism can be thought of as a cut-flower worldview. Once a flower is cut off from the source of its nourishment, it is only a matter of time before it dies. Likewise, humanism bases itself on human value but has cut itself off from the source of human value.

Humanism sees self-reliance as an ultimate virtue. The Bible depicts self-reliance as the original sin. The first humans could not resist the temptation to "be like God" (Gen. 3:5). As the notorious atheist Friedrich Nietzsche put it, "If there were gods, how could I bear not to be a God?"[1]

In sharp contrast to ultimately relying on ourselves, Christianity teaches that the only way for us to truly live is to remove ourselves from the equation. The funeral at which real life begins for each of us is the burying of one's own pride and self-sufficiency. Self-reliance or God-reliance is the simple life-defining choice that every heart has to make.

How has self-reliance failed you?

Humanism can be attractive to people who sense that eternity is written on their hearts (see Eccl. 3:11) and who recognize the human need for meaning, value, purpose, and hope but have been put off by Christianity because they have misconceptions about who God is.

What are the most common misconceptions about God that you have encountered?

How have Christians at times been complicit in fostering misconceptions about God?

How does humanism creep into the Christian life? What do we say or do that is more humanist than Christian?

Sometimes we can be lulled by the influence of humanism into seeing people not as sinners in need of a Savior but as good people who are making progress on their own and just need to work hard to get a bit better.

How would our lives look different if we really believed humanity is headed for spiritual death and desperately needs to be rescued?

Conversational Goal

Introduce this week's conversational goal.

During the next week ask someone who is not a Christian:

Would you mind if I explained the central message of Christianity to you?

PRAYER

Close your time together with prayer.

Read Proverbs 3:5-6 together. Let's spend some time in prayer together about the conversations we will have this week, leaning on God with all of our hearts and trusting that He will make our paths straight.

CONVERSATIONAL GOAL

Use the following question to engage with a nonbeliever this week.

Our first few conversational goals have focused on asking good questions and being good listeners, thereby enabling us to learn about people in a way that deepens trust and relationship. Often when we ask good questions, listen well, and build trust, an opportunity will present itself for us to share our faith.

During the next week ask someone who is not a Christian:

Would you mind if I explained the central message of Christianity to you?

If it helps, you could write the Christian message in your own words and then read it together with them.

After you have explained the central Christian message, consider these follow-up questions.

Ask the person you are talking with what they found difficult, confusing, or unclear.

Ask if anything you shared was new or surprising to them.

Ask if they have any questions about what you shared.

As Christians, we can sometimes forget that things that seem clear to us may not be clear to people who are not used to thinking in Christian categories. Sometimes we can also use language when talking about faith that may be foreign to non-Christians. These conversations will help us see ways we are being unclear or using inaccessible language, and they give us opportunities to treat people with respect by asking to learn from their perspectives.

As we prepare to share the Christian message with a friend, family member, or colleague, we are in great need of God. He must be the One to lead us to the right person; to prepare that person's heart; and to give us His love for that person, His words to share, and faith and courage to trust Him as we make ourselves vulnerable in this way, remembering that Jesus made Himself vulnerable for us.

JOURNAL

Use this page to reflect on your conversation with a nonbeliever.

Whom did you speak with? What was your overall experience with this conversation?

_____

_____

_____

_____

_____

_____

How willing was the person to have a conversation with you? What obstacles did you encounter?

_____

_____

_____

_____

_____

_____

What insights did you gain about communicating truth with gentleness and respect?

_____

_____

_____

_____

_____

_____

_____

Personal Study 1
Humanism

Imagine that a coworker makes these remarks to you over lunch: "Why do we even need God? I mean, what purpose does He serve? Look at the world around us. There are lots of people like me who don't believe in God, yet we're not murderers or rapists or bad people. We all respect one another without the need for reminders from God. Why do I need God to tell me what's right and wrong? Why do I need Him to find meaning or purpose in life? I already feel that I have plenty of meaning and purpose without Him."

How would you respond?

Think about these claims as you complete these two studies on humanism and relativism. You will revisit this conversation at the end of personal study 2.

Humanity in the Driver's Seat

Self-driving cars are often in the media these days. When reading news articles, we often come across the adjective *autonomous,* as in "autonomous self-driving cars." The description is apt because *autonomous* comes from the Greek words *auto* ("self") and *nomos* ("law"). In other words, these cars are self-governed and independent in a way that excludes the need for human direction.

The Bible is clear that when it comes to God, human beings want to be just like these cars, only more so. As C. S. Lewis wrote:

> *Fallen man is not simply an imperfect creature who needs improvement: he is a rebel who must lay down his arms.*[1]

The inclination of the human heart is toward autonomous self-rule. We want to be a law unto ourselves, including redefining what good and evil mean (see Gen. 3:5-7). This was the choice made by Adam and Eve, and as their children we bear their likeness and share their corruption (see Gen. 5:3).

Humanism begs to differ. The American Humanist Association defines *humanism* as:

> A progressive philosophy of life that, without theism and other supernatural beliefs, affirms our ability and responsibility to lead ethical lives of personal fulfillment that aspire to the greater good of humanity.[2]

No longer is God necessary to guide us in morality, to help us understand what is ultimately good, or to define what it means to be human. We are the autonomous masters of our universe, shaping reality to our will and defining these things ourselves. Humanism insists that we can shoulder this burden on our own, but as a belief system humanism ultimately crumbles under the weight of such a task.

This is because humanism is fundamentally flawed as a worldview. Let's consider four reasons humanism is a doomed venture, based on the motivations of the human heart.

REASON 1: HUMANISM IS PROUD

The underlying motivation of pride is likely humanism's biggest flaw. While God "opposes the proud but shows favor to the humble" (1 Pet. 5:5), humanism embraces pride. Consider the following passage from the Humanist Manifesto III.

> Knowledge of the world is derived by observation, experimentation, and rational analysis. … We aspire to this vision with the informed conviction that humanity has the ability to progress toward its highest ideals. The responsibility for our lives and the kind of world in which we live is ours and ours alone.[3]

These words smack of unbridled optimism in human potential. Not only can humanity "progress toward its highest ideals," but it can also do so "without theism and other supernatural beliefs," based on its own rational resources. However, this is not confidence but pride. This sort of thinking is eerily similar to that of the civil engineers who constructed the Tower of Babel:

> Come, let us build ourselves a city, with a tower that reaches to the heavens, so that we may make a name for ourselves.
> **GENESIS 11:4**

The humanist's belief that "responsibility for our lives and the kind of world in which we live is ours and ours alone" is little different in concept from the builders' desire to "make a name for ourselves." Both mentalities are prideful because they suggest that humanity can be great without God. Such a notion is directly refuted throughout the Bible. In fact, this mindset—"I can be the god of my own existence"—is what led to Satan's rebellion (see Isa. 14:12-14; Ezek. 28:17) and humanity's fall (see Gen. 3:5).

Read the following passages and record what they say about the possibility of achieving greatness apart from God.

"My thoughts are not your thoughts,
neither are your ways my ways,"
declares the LORD.
"As the heavens are higher than the earth,
so are my ways higher than your ways
and my thoughts than your thoughts."
ISAIAH 55:8-9

To those who by persistence in doing good seek glory, honor and immortality, he will give eternal life. But for those who are self-seeking and who reject the truth and follow evil, there will be wrath and anger.
ROMANS 2:7-8

If greatness apart from God is not possible, why is this something we sometimes long for?

When have you wanted to be great without God?

REASON 2: HUMANISM LACKS MORAL HUMILITY

As the apostle Paul explained, we each have God's objective moral law written on our heart (see Rom. 2:14-15). By contrast, the American Humanist Association's motto is "Good without a God." In particular, the Humanist Manifesto III asserts the following.

> Ethical values are derived from human need and interest as tested by experience. Humanists ground values in human welfare shaped by human circumstances, interests, and concerns. ... We are committed to treating each person as having inherent worth and dignity, and to making informed choices in a context of freedom consonant with responsibility.[4]

Such flowery language about "inherent worth and dignity" and "freedom consonant with responsibility" certainly sounds nice. Indeed, these are valid ideals that find expression in the Bible. However, humanism demonstrates its lack of moral humility in two ways.

1. Humanism fails to adequately account for the condition of the human heart. No acknowledgment is made of the fact that humans have a natural propensity toward evil, sin, and destruction. We are not upright moral beings. This fact is often challenged, but consider that the twentieth century was among the most violent in all of recorded history, with hundreds of millions of people murdered at the hands of oppressive government regimes As genocide researchers have confirmed, a potential moral monster lurks inside each one of us. Here the Bible and human experience are in agreement with one another.

Read the following passages and record the ways they describe the dire condition of the human heart.

> Surely I was sinful at birth,
> sinful from the time my mother conceived me.
> **PSALM 51:5**

> The heart is deceitful above all things
> and beyond cure.
> Who can understand it?
> **JEREMIAH 17:9**

All have sinned and fall short of the glory of God, and all are justified
freely by his grace through the redemption that came by Christ Jesus.
ROMANS 3:23-24

In what ways do we resist the notion that we are sinful rebels?

Can we really say someone is a great person? Why or why not?

2. Humanism errs in deriving objective moral values such as "inherent worth and dignity" from "human need and interest." We cannot be the moral lawgiver who supplies objective moral values, because we are immoral rebels who are unable to transcend ourselves or our sinful state.

Supposing that we can rise above ourselves by imputing a transcendent quality to our "need and interest as tested by experience" is the height of arrogance. It is to remake God in our own image, which the apostle Paul warned against in the strongest terms:

Although they knew God, they neither glorified him as God nor gave thanks
to him, but their thinking became futile and their foolish hearts were darkened.
Although they claimed to be wise, they became fools and exchanged the glory
of the immortal God for images made to look like a mortal human being. They
exchanged the truth about God for a lie, and worshiped and served created
things rather than the Creator—who is forever praised. Although they know
God's righteous decree that those who do such things deserve death, they not only
continue to do these very things but also approve of those who practice them.
ROMANS 1:21-23,25,32

We cannot supplant God in this manner, for He is holy and we are not.

Ultimately, the standard of what is right and wrong is not sinful human beings but a holy God. Why must we always consider sin from His perspective?

Where in your life are you most tempted to choose your own perspective on sin over God's? What drives you to do this?

Followers of Jesus seek to avoid sin by knowing and obeying God's will.

Jesus replied: " 'Love the Lord your God with all your heart and with all your soul and with all your mind.' This is the first and greatest commandment. And the second is like it: 'Love your neighbor as yourself.' All the Law and the Prophets hang on these two commandments."
MATTHEW 22:37-40

Why is God's will for morality better than the humanistic vision of morality?

Personal Study 2
Relativism and Personhood

Our second study picks up where the first study left off.

REASON 3: HUMANISM UNDERMINES PERSONHOOD

The Humanist Manifesto III makes clear that humanism is a work in progress, but nonetheless, human beings are worthy of dignity and respect:

> *The lifestance [belief system] of Humanism—guided by reason, inspired by compassion, and informed by experience—encourages us to live life well and fully. It evolved through the ages and continues to develop through the efforts of thoughtful people who recognize that values and ideals, however carefully wrought, are subject to change as our knowledge and understandings advance. ... Humanists are concerned for the well being of all, are committed to diversity, and respect those of differing yet humane views. We work to uphold the equal enjoyment of human rights and civil liberties in an open, secular society and maintain it is a civic duty to participate in the democratic process.[1]*

Here is the problem. What happens when those who accept or sympathize with humanism change their minds and are no longer interested in being "thoughtful" or "concerned for the well being of all"? What happens if the humanist "values and ideals," which are "subject to change," are replaced with new norms that do not "uphold the equal enjoyment of rights and civil liberties"? In short, what happens when a revolution of ideas takes hold and the outcome is not so favorable?

For example, suppose someone takes to heart Richard Dawkins's claim that the universe has "no design, no purpose, no evil and no good"[2] or experiences the same "epiphany" as atheist philosopher Joel Marks that "without God, there is no morality."[3] Given the wretched condition of the human heart, what harvest of evil conduct might such corrupt soil yield in the end? Judging by the past century of death and bloodshed, authoritarian regimes, genocide, and the devaluing of humans are possible outcomes. Humanism that lacks a transcendent, value-giving authority can be easily toppled by a change of human will. The reason is simple: no one is ever right or wrong.

Without God each of us is his or her own king or queen, and we step into the realm of the purely subjective, where phrases like "intrinsic value" and "equal authority" have no real meaning.

> **God created all of us with objective purpose and meaning (see Gen. 1:28-31). Why must we always determine our worth based on the objective standard of God's Word?**

> **What happens when we derive our sense of purpose and meaning from another source?**

In a purely humanistic world even the very concept of personhood can be lost. In Jesus' time only a Roman citizen was considered a true person. David Bentley Hart notes that we now use the word *person* with "a splendidly indiscriminate generosity, applying it without hesitation to everyone, regardless of social station, race, or sex."[4] But this practice exists only because of the influence of Christianity. If we jettison God, as humanism encourages, then there is no reason governments cannot once again become the dispensers of personhood, granting it to some and denying it to others. Indeed, this is America's own legal heritage as recently as 1856.[5]

In short, humanism not only relativizes morality but also opens the door to the relativization of personhood. As Os Guinness explains:

> *Man made only in the image of Man loses his and her inviolability, for dignity that is self-created is weaker than dignity that is conferred. Mere existence does not add up to human dignity. ... Only if humans are made in the image of God—may they be physically and mentally handicapped, socially degraded or educationally deprived—can they always and irrevocably have a precious and inalienable dignity that none may abrogate or harm.[6]*

Thus, the only true humanism that objectively affirms human existence, dignity, and personhood is Christian humanism. The Bible reveals that these cherished values are grounded not in human consensus, reason, or experience (see Rom. 12:2; 1 John 2:15-17) but in God Himself.

> **What does each of the following verses reveal about human equality, purpose, or meaning? How does each demonstrate that these ideas are rooted in God? Record your observations.**
>
> **Equality and unity: Galatians 3:28; Philippians 2:3-7**
>
> **Dignity: Genesis 1:26-27; 9:6**
>
> **Purpose and meaning: Psalm 8:6-8**
>
> **Intentionality and design: Psalm 139:13-16**

REASON 4: HUMANISM MISPLACES ITS HOPE FOR THE FUTURE

When it comes to death, humanism puts on a brave face. As the Humanist Manifesto III remarks:

> *We accept our life as all and enough, distinguishing things as they are from things as we might wish or imagine them to be. … We aim for our fullest possible development and animate our lives with a deep sense of purpose, finding wonder and awe in the joys and beauties of human existence, its challenges and tragedies, and even in the inevitability and finality of death.*[7]

Indeed, such a glib attitude is the humanist's only real option because humanists cannot offer hope beyond the material world. The humanist hope is really a futile attempt to reconstruct reality according to personal wishes. But saying it does not make it so.

In reality, there is no "wonder and awe ... in the inevitability and finality of death" for the two following reasons.

1. Human death is the result of humankind's rebellion (see Gen. 2:17; Rom. 5:12).

   Read the following verses about death and fill in the blanks.

   Romans 6:23; James 1:15: _____ leads to death.

   1 Corinthians 15:26: At the end of time, when heaven is ushered in, the last enemy to be destroyed will be _____ itself.

   2 Timothy 1:10: _____ has destroyed death.

   Revelation 1:18: _____ holds the keys to death in His hands.

   Revelation 20:14; 21:4: Death will ultimately be thrown into the _____ and will be no more.

   Who among your friends would not recognize the link between sin and death?

   What dangers come from failing to recognize the cause of death?

Sin is both our enemy and God's enemy. Therefore, the apostle Paul dared to taunt death because of his victory through Christ:

> *When the perishable has been clothed with the imperishable,*
> *and the mortal with immortality, then the saying that is written*
> *will come true: "Death has been swallowed up in victory."*
> *"Where, O death, is your victory?*
> *Where, O death, is your sting?"*
> *The sting of death is sin, and the power of sin is the law. But thanks*
> *be to God! He gives us the victory through our Lord Jesus Christ.*
> **1 CORINTHIANS 15:54-57**

2. Death was never meant to be wonderful. Death is a punishment for sin and rebellion, but for people who trust in Jesus Christ, death is anything but final. Because of Jesus' death and resurrection, death will not have the last word. Jesus taught that we are soulish beings—a functional unity of body and soul—not just material, biological machines (see Matt. 10:28).

In short, we are not headed for death and injustice but for greater and greater life. Not only has death been overcome, but we will also reign with God "for ever and ever" (Rev. 22:5) as "a royal priesthood" (1 Pet. 2:9). Professor Clay Jones summarizes this truth well:

> *God is giving us the kingdom and not just any kingdom, but the kingdom.*
> *And once Jesus comes, there will be no other. We get it all. ... We get it all. ... He is giving us*
> *a controlling interest in part of heaven. He talks about ruling cities, He talks*
> *about true riches, He tells us to be faithful over things here. ... Truly. Big.*
> *Things. Come. We are going to reign over them, and we are going to do this*
> *with Jesus. That is God's plan for our lives, and it has always been the plan.*[8]

That is the kind of eternity that deserves our "wonder and awe," one in which we can be "set free in [God's] universe, empowered to do what we want to do and were made to do."[9]

Some people claim it is possible to create heaven or a utopia here on earth apart from God. Take a moment to read Psalm 118:9; 146:3; and Proverbs 27:1. Why would it be a mistake to put our hope in a future utopia founded solely on human efforts?

Jesus conquered sin and death by enduring suffering. If Jesus overcame Satan and evil through suffering, should we expect that our path will be any different (see Eph. 6:12)?

How does a humanistic worldview fail to offer hope during hardship and difficulty?

How should this knowledge, along with the eternal splendor of heaven that awaits us, help us endure suffering in this life?

Look at the questions your coworker asked on page 74. How could you respond to your coworker's humanistic claims differently in light of what you have learned this week?

How does a Christian worldview give greater purpose and meaning to life than a humanistic worldview?

For further study read the articles on pages 139–42.

WEEK 5
Hedonism

START

Use the following content to begin group session 5. Start by discussing last week's conversational goal.

In your conversations this past week, you asked a nonbeliever:

> Would you mind if I explained the central message of Christianity to you?

Were people willing to hear the Christian message?

How did people respond after hearing the Christian message? What did people find confusing, difficult, or unclear about what you shared? What did people find new or surprising? What questions did they have?

Were you encouraged or discouraged (or both) by this experience of sharing the Christian message? In what ways?

In light of your conversations, how would you change the way you share the Christian message next time?

THIS WEEK'S TOPIC

Use this page to introduce this week's topic.

Hedonism is the view that life is all about happiness or pleasure. Imagine there were a machine that would give you any experience you desired (maybe before long there will be!). You could choose to experience winning Olympic gold, falling in love, or making a great scientific discovery, and the neurons in your brain would be stimulated in such a way that you would experience a simulation of actually doing these things. Although in reality you would be floating in a tank of goo with electrodes hooked up to your brain, you would be experiencing total pleasure.[1]

> *Given the choice, would you preprogram your experiences and plug into this machine? Why or why not?*

> *A lot of people say, "I don't need God; I'm happy as I am." What would you say in response?*

> *Is pleasure a good thing? Do you think God wants us to be happy? Explain.*

WATCH

Watch video session 5.

HEDONISM: *life is all about happiness or pleasure.*

*Anything that refreshes you and delights you in life is a legitimate
pleasure so long as it does not violate your ultimate purpose in life.*

RAVI ZACHARIAS

*Happiness as a philosophy of life seems to be incredibly exclusive.
So much of the world is not in a position to adopt that philosophy of life.*

VINCE VITALE

*All pleasure comes at a cost. For the right kind of pleasure, you pay the price before
you enjoy it. For the wrong kind of pleasure, you pay the price after you enjoy it.*

RAVI ZACHARIAS

*Is it the case that atheists are generally happy, or is it
that we tend without God to just be distracted?*

VINCE VITALE

*God is not against pleasure. He just wants us to find it in the right way and the
right purpose, and that right purpose is by the rules for which God has made us.*

RAVI ZACHARIAS

*This isn't just a problem outside the church. This is a problem
inside the church as well. Hedonism creeps into the church.*

VINCE VITALE

*Hedonism is something to which we are naturally drawn,
but like the devil himself, ultimately it leaves you emptier
than before. Only in Christ is true fulfillment found.*

RAVI ZACHARIAS

DISCUSS

Use the following questions to discuss the video session.

Happiness and pleasure are good things, but when we make happiness and pleasure the highest forms of good, we risk missing out on the best God has for us.

If you had to choose one word or phrase to express what constitutes a good life, what would it be? Why?

In the video Ravi pointed out that all pleasure comes at a cost. For the right kind of pleasure, we pay for it before we have enjoyed it. For the wrong kind of pleasure, we pay for it after we have enjoyed it.

What are some examples of the truth of these statements?

The temptation of hedonism is also a problem in the church. Sometimes we settle for far less than God has for us. Imagine that a young boy traveled for twenty-seven hours through flight delays to get to Disney World. After finally arriving in Florida, he looked at the revolving baggage-claim carousel, which to him looked like a ride, and exclaimed, "Thanks, Dad! I love Disney World!" This boy was Vince's brother, Jay. He was too quick to settle for so much less than his father had in store for him.

In what ways do we tend to settle for cheap, temporary imitations rather than for the fullness of what God desires for us?

How has hedonism failed you?

In what ways could advances in technology (for example, virtual reality, augmented reality, and artificial intelligence) intensify the temptations to choose pleasure over what is good and true in the years ahead?

Was Jesus a hedonist? In what ways does Jesus' life challenge a hedonistic perspective?

How is the life to which Jesus calls us different from hedonism?

Conversational Goal

Introduce this week's conversational goal.

During the next week ask someone who is not a Christian:

Would it be all right if I prayed for you?

After you have finished praying, ask your friend what they thought about the experience of prayer. Tell them that you will continue to pray for their requests.

PRAYER

Close your time together with prayer.

God says we do not need to spend our time in an endless, exhausting pursuit of pleasure (see Ps. 16:11). He is the One who can fill us with joy, and that joy is found when we rest in His presence.

> *Take a minute in silence to identify one specific way we have personally been living like hedonists, chasing pleasure without considering the cost rather than counting the cost as followers of Jesus Christ. Write down your thoughts in the space provided.*

Let's finish this week's session by reading Psalm 51:1-17 together as a prayer of reliance on God's mercy and love and as an expression of our desire to find joy in Him. Consider reading these verses aloud as a group, taking turns as each member reads one verse.

CONVERSATIONAL GOAL

Use the following question to engage with a nonbeliever this week.

The Bible tells us that prayer is "powerful and effective" (Jas. 5:16). It is challenging to reflect on whether we really believe that statement and whether our disciplines of prayer reflect this truth.

This week's conversational goal is to tell someone who is not yet a Christian that you believe prayer makes a difference and that you would like to pray for them.

During the next week ask someone who is not a Christian:

Would it be all right if I prayed for you?

If they are, ask them what their current needs are. What are they currently hoping for or struggling with? Ask if you can pray for them right then in person.

Someone once said that there are two ways to choose a coat. You can check all of the dimensions of the coat, or you can try it on. Both ways are important. Many people are not even willing to consider the possibility of God unless they can see that the dimensions—the evidence of science, philosophy, and history—at least point in God's direction. But ultimately, if someone wants to know God, there is no substitute for encountering Him directly. In His generosity God has given us the gift of prayer so that we can do just that. For some people, experiencing prayer may be a key step on their journey toward trusting God and being clothed in Christ.

After you have finished praying, ask your friend what they thought about the experience of prayer. Tell them that you will continue to pray for their requests.

JOURNAL

Use this page to reflect on your conversation with a nonbeliever.

Whom did you speak with? What was your overall experience with this conversation?

_____

_____

_____

_____

_____

_____

How willing was the person to have a conversation with you? What obstacles did you encounter?

_____

_____

_____

_____

_____

_____

What insights did you gain about communicating truth with gentleness and respect?

_____

_____

_____

_____

_____

_____

Personal Study 1
Pleasure

Imagine you are out to dinner and overhear this conversation at the next table: "Suppose God does exist. Even if that's true and He sets the rules about morality, why would I want to worship Him? Why would I want to spend eternity with someone so, well, boring? He cares only about rules. He's no fun; He's anti-pleasure, anti-enjoyment, and anti-happiness. Why else would He prohibit all of the enjoyable things in life? Why would I want to be condemned to an eternity of boredom?"

How would you respond?

Think about these claims as you complete these two studies on hedonism. You will come back to this conversation at the end of personal study 2.

God Is Pro-pleasure

Christianity has an undeserved bad reputation when it comes to pleasure. For example, Mark Twain wrote, "Choose heaven for the climate and hell for the company."[1] The reality is far different; God's kingdom is not the home of nerds and prudes. Contrary to our culture's popular opinion, God is actually pro-pleasure. This statement may sound surprising, but it is true. The fact that God is pro-pleasure is an important but overlooked component of the gospel.

To our culture, the decision to trust Christ is a decision to renounce pleasure altogether, which makes spending eternity in heaven with God sound like a punishment rather than a reward. Consider the following examples.

- The Irish playwright George Bernard Shaw, who won the Nobel Prize in Literature in 1925, wrote, "Heaven, as conventionally conceived, is a place so inane, so dull, so useless, so miserable, that nobody has ever ventured to describe a whole day in heaven."[2]
- Actor Jack Nicholson admits, "I always said, 'Hey, you can have whatever rules you want—I'm going to have mine. I'll accept the guilt. I'll pay the check. I'll do the time.'"[3]

- Mark Twain's letter to his wife is remarkable: "I am plenty safe enough in his hands; I am not in any danger from that kind of a Deity. The one that I want to keep out of the reach of is the caricature of him which one finds in the Bible. We (that one and I) could never respect each other, never get along together. I have met his superior a hundred times—In fact I amount to that myself."[4]

These conclusions are unfortunate, because the same God who made "the heavens and the earth" (Gen. 1:1) also made delicious food, the sensation of jumping into cool water on a hot day, sunrises and sunsets, and even sex—and He called them all good. Heaven will be full of murderers (Moses), adulterers (David), terrorists (Paul), thieves (see Luke 23:40-43), and prostitutes (Rahab) who repented of their sin and chose to enjoy an eternity of pleasure with God.

Scripture often depicts our reunion with Jesus as a banquet (see Isa. 25:6; Matt. 22:2; 25:1-10; Mark 14:25; Rev. 19:9) and a joyful party (see Luke 15:11-32). Moreover, Jesus ate so often with sinners that the Pharisees accused Him of being "a glutton and a drunkard" (Matt. 11:19). That is not a God who is anti-pleasure!

Understanding Pleasure

In C. S. Lewis's classic work *The Screwtape Letters* a senior demon (Screwtape) writes a series of letters to his nephew (Wormwood) to assist him in securing the damnation of a man known as "the Patient" (God is referred to as "the Enemy"). The following passage is telling.

Never forget that when we are dealing with any pleasure in its healthy and normal and satisfying form, we are, in a sense, on the Enemy's ground. I know we have won many a soul through pleasure. All the same, it is His invention, not ours. He made the pleasures: all our research so far has not enabled us to produce one. All we can do is encourage the humans to take the pleasures which our Enemy has produced, at times, or in ways, or in degrees, which He has forbidden. Hence we always try to work away from the natural condition of any pleasure to that in which it is least natural, least redolent of its Maker, and least pleasurable. An ever increasing craving for an ever diminishing pleasure is the formula.[5]

Do you think of pleasure as being unchristian? Why is this not the case?

What is an example of a pleasure God has intended for our good that leads to sin when it becomes ultimate?

Although God is pro-pleasure, He is opposed to the misuse of pleasure because of its negative effects. And that is the very risk of pleasure—its abuse. God is the Creator of all legitimate earthly pleasures, but through sin we have a natural tendency to crave illegitimate pleasures. Because the human heart has a way of corrupting legitimate pleasures into illegitimate pursuits, it is critical to understand how to handle pleasure from a biblical perspective. We will look at three important principles in this regard.

PRINCIPLE 1: ONLY TEMPORARY PLEASURE IS FOUND IN THIS WORLD.
In the movie *The Avengers,* when asked by Captain America what he is without his Iron Man armor, Tony Stark quips, "Genius, billionaire, playboy, philanthropist." King Solomon was all of those and more.

Read the following verses and fill in the details about Solomon's life.

1 Kings 4:23: Solomon's daily provision of meat included _____ cattle.

1 Kings 4:26: Solomon owned _____ horses at a time when animals equated to wealth.

1 Kings 4:32: Solomon spoke _____ proverbs and composed _____ songs.

1 Kings 11:3: Solomon had _____ wives and _____ concubines.

By the standards of his day, Solomon "was greater in riches and wisdom than all the other kings of the earth" (1 Kings 10:23), and "his fame spread to all the surrounding nations," so that "people came to listen to Solomon's wisdom, sent by all the kings of the world" (4:31,34). He lived in a palace that took thirteen years to construct (see 7:1) and in which everything was made of gold "because silver was considered of little value in Solomon's days" (10:21).

Even by the most decadent of modern standards, Solomon had all this world can offer: feasting, sex, money, fame, power, security, and wisdom. Yet here is what he concluded after fully enjoying these earthly delights:

> *I denied myself nothing my eyes desired;*
> *I refused my heart no pleasure.*
> *My heart took delight in all my labor,*
> *and this was the reward for all my toil.*
> *Yet when I surveyed all that my hands had done*
> *and what I had toiled to achieve,*
> *everything was meaningless, a chasing after the wind;*
> *nothing was gained under the sun.*
> **ECCLESIASTES 2:10-11**

It is important to understand that the phrase "under the sun" (v. 11) is a Hebrew expression for "without God." As Ravi has written, paraphrasing G. K. Chesterton, "Meaninglessness does not come from being weary of pain. Meaninglessness comes from being weary of pleasure."[6] Solomon understood that no pleasure in this world is lasting, and therefore an abundance of pleasure can lead to meaninglessness. The things of this world are not worth loving as God ought to be loved, for the world and its desires will pass away (see 1 John 2:15-17).

Os Guinness writes, "An endless proliferation of trivial and unworthy choices is not freedom but slavery by another name. ... Freedom is not the permission to do what we like but the power to do what we should."[7] Do you think this is an accurate definition of freedom? Why or why not?

What instances can you identify in which this truth was highlighted?

Personal Study 2
Surviving Pleasure before Eternity

For this second study we pick up where the first study ended.

PRINCIPLE 2: PLEASURE CAN BE AN IDOL THAT DIMINISHES OUR RELATIONSHIP WITH GOD, DERAILS OUR LIVES, AND DISTRACTS FROM GOD'S PURPOSES. Recall that this is precisely Screwtape's advice to Wormwood: "All we can do is encourage the humans to take the pleasures which [God] has produced, at times, or in ways, or in degrees, which He has forbidden." The dangers of abusing pleasure are numerous.

> *Read the following verses and identify some of the negative effects of abusing pleasure.*
>
> *Spiritual: Luke 8:14*
>
> *Financial: Proverbs 21:17*
>
> *Prayer: James 4:3*
>
> *Righteousness: 2 Timothy 3:4*
>
> *Quality of life: 1 Timothy 6:9*
>
> *Freedom: Titus 3:3*

Ultimately, an unrighteous, sinful abuse of pleasure can lead to a spiritual calcification of the heart, a depraved mind, a rejection of legitimate authority, a degradation of the body, and an act of divine judgment in which God gives the sinner over to his or her self-destruction (see Rom. 1:21-32; 2 Pet. 2).

Once again, God is pro-pleasure, but He is opposed to the misuse of pleasure because of the inherent dangers involved. Hedonism is an affliction of the heart that requires a supernatural remedy (see Ezek. 36:26). Even so, we have a significant part to play in our sanctification.

Exactly how does someone enjoy legitimate pleasures without allowing them to become snares, idols, or distractions? Enjoying legitimate pleasures within God's reasonable limits is a matter of wisdom, self-discipline, and at times supernatural assistance from the Holy Spirit. In this regard, the Bible offers five critical words of instruction.

1. *Feed yourself well.* The abuse of pleasure in this life can be avoided by storing what is good, noble, holy, worthwhile, and righteous in our hearts (see Ps. 119:9-11; Matt. 15:18-20; Eph. 5:15-20).
2. *Practice self-control.* Pleasure must be handled in moderation (see Prov. 25:16), and the temptation to abuse it must be mastered (see Gen. 4:7; 1 Pet. 5:8-9). Godly leaders gladly choose to suffer along with the people of God rather than enjoy the fleeting pleasures of sin (see 2 Tim. 2:22).
3. *Pursue sexual purity.* Each of us should honor marriage and sexuality as God designed them. Sexual immorality and lust are the results of our fallen sinful nature and are therefore contrary to God's holiness (see Rom. 13:13; 1 Cor. 6:9-20; Gal. 5:19-21; Eph. 5:3; Col. 3:5-6; 1 Thess. 4:3; 1 Tim. 1:9-10; Heb. 13:4).
4. *Delight in what is best.* Feed something and it will grow; starve something and it will die. The righteous who delight in God's Word will receive wisdom and prosper like a tree planted by streams of water (see Ps. 1:1-3; 119:127-131).
5. *Understand the big picture.* Jesus calls His followers to sacrificial love rather than the evasion of pain or the exhausting pursuit of pleasure (see Luke 9:23; John 15:20; Phil 1:29; 3:10-11).

Of the previous instructions, which do you find the hardest to put into practice?

Read Philippians 4:8. Do you take Paul's advice into account when selecting movies or TV shows to watch, music to download, books to read, and other entertainment to enjoy? Why or why not?

How can the things you enjoy become a means for you to enjoy God?

PRINCIPLE 3: ETERNAL AND ULTIMATELY FULFILLING PLEASURE IS FOUND IN A RELATIONSHIP WITH GOD.

C. S. Lewis wrote:

> *Scripture and tradition habitually put the joys of heaven into the scale against the sufferings of earth, and no solution of the problem of pain that does not do so can be called a Christian one.[1]*

Indeed, the joys of heaven and the pleasures that await us there are additional components of the gospel that deserve significant attention.

In week 1 we reflected on the meaning of life: Why do we exist? Now that you have completed five weeks of Bible study, try to answer this question in just a few sentences.

The Westminster Shorter Catechism summarizes the meaning of life this way: "Man's chief end is to glorify God, and to enjoy him forever."[2] How does your answer compare?

The promises of Scripture reflect this purpose for humankind. Consider the following biblical teachings.

- God Himself is the reward for a life of faith (see Gen. 15:1).
- God will fill us with joy in His presence and eternal pleasures at His right hand (see Ps. 16:11).
- Those who delight themselves in the Lord will receive the desires of their hearts (see Ps. 37:4).
- Following God leads us to sacrificial love and service of others, which bring not only pleasure but also fullness of life (see John 10:10).
- God promises a hundredfold to people who make sacrifices for Him (see Mark 10:29-30).
- Jesus gave up heavenly comfort and luxury to come to earth and live in human poverty so that we could become rich (see Rom. 8:17; 2 Cor. 8:9).
- Happiness is a gift of God, who fills our hearts with joy (see Acts 14:17).

Philosopher Richard Swinburne writes:

> Friendship with God [is] of supreme value, for he is (by definition) perfectly good and, being (by definition) omnipotent and omniscient, will ever be able to hold our interest by showing us new facets of reality and above all his own nature.[3]

In heaven we will enjoy God through our friendship with Him, and we will glorify God because of who He is and the wonder with which He will fill our imaginations for all eternity. That is the ultimate, everlasting pleasure!

What does it mean to say that heaven is primarily a person rather than a place? Why should we not want heaven if God was not there?

How could you now respond to the conversation you overheard at the restaurant (p. 94)? Is God anti-pleasure? In what ways is God actually pro-pleasure?

For further study read the articles on pages 143–47.

WEEK 6
Conversations That Count

START

Use the following content to begin group session 6. Start by discussing last week's conversational goal.

Over the last week you were challenged to ask a nonbeliever:

> Would it be all right if I prayed for you?

How did your conversations go this past week?

Was your friend open to being prayed for? What was his or her response to being prayed for?

What did you learn from this experience?

In what types of future situations could you offer to pray for non-Christians?

Continue to pray for your friend's requests and to follow up with him or her about these concerns. God has heard your prayer and is at work.

THIS WEEK'S TOPIC

Use this page to introduce this week's topic.

Jesus' final charge to His disciples was:

> *Go and make disciples of all nations, baptizing them in the name of the Father and of the Son and of the Holy Spirit, and teaching them to obey everything I have commanded you.*
>
> **MATTHEW 28:19-20**

> *You will receive power when the Holy Spirit comes on you; and you will be my witnesses in Jerusalem, and in all Judea and Samaria, and to the ends of the earth.*
>
> **ACTS 1:8**

A lot of Christians want to honor Jesus' final wishes by sharing the gospel with others, but they find doing so intimidating and do not know where to start. We have learned that an excellent place to start is by taking conversation seriously as a spiritual discipline and as a key aspect of Christian discipleship. That is why we included a conversational goal in each week of this study.

Jesus was a superb conversationalist. In all of the Gospels we see that Jesus spent a lot of time talking with people, and it is not at all unreasonable to think He had as great an impact through His conversational ministry as through His preaching ministry. It is surprising, therefore, that growing as a conversationalist is rarely mentioned in discussions of what it means to follow Jesus.

Why do you think we don't take developing as conversationalists as seriously as we take other aspects of Christian discipleship?

One reason we often find it difficult to move conversations from shooting the breeze to talking about Jesus is that we spend so much of our conversational time merely shooting the breeze. Nothing is wrong with shooting the breeze, but Jesus always made the transition to deep, meaningful conversations. Like Him, we need to spend more of our time conversing about meaningful topics, especially spiritual ones.

How can we develop the habit of spending more of our time in meaningful conversations?

What are some meaningful topics we could discuss that might lead to conversations about spiritual truth?

WATCH
Watch video session 6.

Jesus spent a lot of time in conversations with people.
VINCE VITALE

Find something that person cares about. There's something
they care about that you could invest in.
VINCE VITALE

Be a good reader of history or novels, which are conversation pieces.
RAVI ZACHARIAS

If you are fearful of a subject, you will never enter
a conversation with a hardened skeptic.
RAVI ZACHARIAS

"I don't know" is a great answer.
VINCE VITALE

Be a better question asker and be a better responder to questions.
VINCE VITALE

If you're a churchgoing Christian, the question "How was your
weekend?" is an absolute gift that we just pass up all the time.
VINCE VITALE

A conversation is a means of establishing a trusted relationship.
RAVI ZACHARIAS

Asking questions is a good way to lead into opening the heart of a person.
RAVI ZACHARIAS

If I were to ask you what keeps you from giving your life
to Jesus Christ, what would your answer be?
RAVI ZACHARIAS

Video sessions available at lifeway.com/jesusamongseculargods
or with a subscription to smallgroup.com

DISCUSS

Use the following questions to discuss the video session.

God knew that the best way to establish a relationship with humanity was literally to come and speak our language. In the video Vince shared that he began watching the New York Yankees in order to speak his dad's language, and Ravi told how his mother learned about ice hockey in order to speak the language of her student.

> *What is one way you could invest in the interests of someone with whom you would like to share the gospel, as a way of loving them and deepening your relationship with them?*

BE QUESTION-READY. Jesus asked a lot of good questions (one estimate is that 307 of them are recorded in the New Testament), but our most common questions tend to lack creativity: "How was your weekend?" "Did you have a good summer?" "How's it going?" "How's work?" These are questions that can be and usually are answered in three words or less, without any meaningful information being shared.

> *Read "Questions That Count" on pages 122–23. What questions do you like? What do you like about them?*
>
> *What are some other meaningful questions you could add to this list?*

BE RESPONSE-READY. When Jesus responded to a question, He did so very discerningly and purposefully: "Why do you call me good?" (Mark 10:18). "Give back to Caesar what is Caesar's, and to God what is God's" (Matt. 22:21). "Let any one of you who is without sin be the first to throw a stone" (John 8:7).

Maybe one reason Jesus was able to respond with such wisdom and intentionality is that He prayed about the questions and challenges He saw coming. We also know many of the questions we are asked regularly or will be asked in various situations. Will we take time to be prepared to respond in meaningful ways that can lead to conversations that count?

> *What is a question you are often asked that you generally respond to in a routine way?*
>
> *How could we respond to those questions in creative ways that could lead to meaningful conversations?*

When we respond meaningfully to everyday questions, we build the depth of relationship from which people will be more likely to ask us questions about our faith. As we trust God for deeper conversations in our daily lives and people begin to ask difficult questions, it is important to remember that "I don't know" is a valid answer. People do not want to join a community of know-it-alls. People want to join a community that cares enough to take their question seriously, do some research, and come back with a thoughtful response and an invitation to continue the conversation.

BE INVITATIONAL. Vince pointed out on the video that people usually do not show up at a party if they have not received invitations. Moreover, receiving an invitation to a party is a gift, even if the person who is invited decides that he or she is unable to attend.

> *Why do you think we tend to be hesitant about inviting people into the Christian life—to the party God is throwing?*

Will you accept God's invitation to be involved in inviting people into relationships with Him? If you do, you will be surprised by how many people will say yes to your invitations, and you will know the incomparable joy of seeing the light go on in their eyes when they begin to see Jesus for who He really is and to appreciate the fullness of life that only He can bring.

Conversational Goal
Introduce this week's conversational goal.

During the next week ask someone who is not a Christian:

**If I asked you what keeps you from giving
your life to Jesus, what would you say?**

PRAYER
Close your time together with prayer.

Read Romans 1:16. Then lead your group in a time of silent prayer asking God to bring to mind anyone in your life to whom He wants you to extend His invitation to know and follow Him in a life-giving relationship. Commit to pray daily during the coming week for the other people in your group and for God to bless the invitations they will offer.

CONVERSATIONAL GOAL

Use the following question to engage with a nonbeliever this week.

We hope you have been encouraged and challenged by these weekly conversational goals, and we hope you will make them a part of your everyday life.

These goals are practical ways we can love people well and show our love for them by interacting with them in meaningful ways. For example, if you know you are going to see someone tomorrow, ask God tonight if there is a question He wants you to ask them or if there is a response He wants you to give to a question they always ask you.

During the next week ask someone who is not a Christian:

If I asked you what keeps you from giving your life to Jesus, what would you say?

If they do not identify a significant barrier, ask whether they want to pray, asking God to forgive their sins and telling Him they want to follow Him.

If someone is not ready to take this step, ask if they would be willing to pray a seeker's prayer:

> *God, I'm not sure if You are there, but if You are, I would really like to know it. If You show Yourself to me, I will put my trust in You.*

We have seen God honor this very powerful prayer countless times.

If we all commit to this conversational goal, by this time next week we believe we will have new brothers and sisters in Christ, that eternal destinies will have been transformed!

We do not know which of our invitations will be accepted, but there is power in community. If we each commit to offer one invitation, we will help motivate one another. Regardless of which invitations are accepted, we all will have had the amazing privilege and eternal joy of participating in building God's kingdom.

JOURNAL

Use this page to reflect on your conversation with a nonbeliever.

Whom did you speak with? What was your overall experience with this conversation?

_____

_____

_____

_____

_____

_____

How willing was the person to have a conversation with you? What obstacles did you encounter?

_____

_____

_____

_____

_____

_____

What insights did you gain about communicating truth with gentleness and respect?

_____

_____

_____

_____

_____

_____

Personal Study 1
Relational Networks

Living as Insiders

As Jim Petersen and Mike Shamy explain in their book *The Insider*,[1] each of us is one of God's insiders among our family members, friends, neighbors, coworkers, and social networks. As insiders, we play an indispensable role in working out God's purposes, because each of us has inside access to a unique set of relationships through which the gospel can organically move and advance.

Insiders are key people involved in bringing the gospel to a family, a marketplace, or any other social context through natural relationships. The beauty of this ministry concept is that it does not require going anywhere new or joining a program. An insider's ministry is never far away because it occurs through daily life and conversation.

Sound too easy? Certainly, an effective insider ministry takes time and intentionality. Jesus did not just eat and drink with sinners and tax collectors (see Matt. 11:19); He lingered with them, spending quality time serving and ministering to them. And an insider must do the same. However, the task is made easier by the fact that the people with whom we are sharing Jesus' gospel of forgiveness and eternal life are not projects or strangers but friends, relatives, colleagues, and peers who already have a meaningful presence in our lives.

The gospel spreads most naturally through relational networks; therefore, a ministry field surrounds each one of us. Recall the following scene from the Gospel of Mark.

> They went across the lake to the region of the Gerasenes. When Jesus got out of the boat, a man with an impure spirit came from the tombs to meet him. ... When he saw Jesus from a distance, he ran and fell on his knees in front of him. He shouted at the top of his voice, "What do you want with me, Jesus, Son of the Most High God? In God's name don't torture me!" For Jesus had said to him, "Come out of this man, you impure spirit!"... A large herd of pigs was feeding on the nearby hillside. The demons begged Jesus, "Send us among the pigs; allow us to go into them." He gave them permission, and the impure spirits came out and went into the pigs. ... When [the people] came to Jesus, they saw the man who had been possessed by the legion of demons, sitting there, dressed and in his right mind; and they were afraid. ...

As Jesus was getting into the boat, the man who had been demon-possessed begged to go with him. Jesus did not let him, but said, "Go home to your own people and tell them how much the Lord has done for you, and how he has had mercy on you." So the man went away and began to tell in the Decapolis how much Jesus had done for him. And all the people were amazed.

MARK 5:1-20

Given his amazing deliverance, the demoniac naturally asked to join Jesus and journey with Him back to Galilee. Jesus' response to his request is instructive. Rather than permit the man to join Him, Jesus sent the demoniac to his "own people" to "tell them how much the Lord" had done for him (v. 19). In other words, Jesus sent the man back to the place where he was an insider. There the man would already be known, and the testimony of his life-changing encounter with Jesus might be more readily accepted.

Make a list of places where you are an insider.

Who in those places most needs to hear about Jesus?

Pause for a moment to pray for them. Consider writing your prayer here.

Come and See

In John 1:35-50 we read an account of Jesus gathering His first disciples. These men did not know much about Jesus at the time, but they perceived enough to take an interest in Him and over time began to follow Him. Let's look at this passage and consider what we can learn about our own witness for Jesus.[2]

The next day John was there again with two of his disciples. When he saw Jesus passing by, he said, "Look, the Lamb of God!" When the two disciples heard him say this, they followed Jesus. Turning around, Jesus saw them following and asked, "What do you want?" They said, "Rabbi" (which means "Teacher"), "where are you staying?" "Come," he replied, "and you will see." So they went and saw where he was staying, and they spent that day with him. It was about four in the afternoon. Andrew, Simon Peter's brother, was one of the two who heard what John had said and who had followed Jesus. The first thing Andrew did was to find his brother Simon and tell him, "We have found the Messiah" (that is, the Christ). And he brought him to Jesus. Jesus looked at him and said, "You are Simon son of John. You will be called Cephas" (which, when translated, is Peter). The next day Jesus decided to leave for Galilee. Finding Philip, he said to him, "Follow me." Philip, like Andrew and Peter, was from the town of Bethsaida. Philip found Nathanael and told him, "We have found the one Moses wrote about in the Law, and about whom the prophets also wrote—Jesus of Nazareth, the son of Joseph." "Nazareth! Can anything good come from there?" Nathanael asked. "Come and see," said Philip. When Jesus saw Nathanael approaching, he said of him, "Here truly is an Israelite in whom there is no deceit." "How do you know me?" Nathanael asked. Jesus answered, "I saw you while you were still under the fig tree before Philip called you." Then Nathanael declared, "Rabbi, you are the Son of God; you are the king of Israel." Jesus said, "You believe because I told you I saw you under the fig tree. You will see greater things than that."

JOHN 1:35-50

Andrew, Simon, Philip, and Nathanael are all introduced to Jesus in this passage. What were their attitudes toward Jesus before meeting Him? What was each man's initial understanding of Jesus?

How was each man introduced to Jesus? What similarities and differences did you observe?

What was each man's reaction to hearing about Jesus?

How did each man respond on meeting Jesus and hearing His words to him? What similarities and differences did you observe?

Think back to the time when someone first invited you to follow Jesus. Who were the key people who helped introduce you to Jesus?

What did they do? What did they say, and how did they say it?

What was your initial reaction and response?

Four key observations can be drawn from this account in which Andrew, Simon, Philip, and Nathanael were introduced to Jesus.

1. *Everyone has a different starting point.* Before being introduced to Jesus, each person had a different attitude, knowledge base, and level of interest. In terms of attitude, Nathanael was clearly skeptical, and Simon may have been as well. In contrast, both Andrew and Philip were quite enthusiastic. In terms of knowledge, Andrew received information about Jesus from John the Baptist, and both Philip and Nathanael seemed to have some knowledge of the Torah.

2. *Personal introductions are important.* Four of the five men in this passage (one is unnamed) were introduced to Jesus by someone else through testimony, invitation, or persuasion. Andrew and another man were introduced by John the Baptist, Simon was introduced by Andrew, and Nathanael was introduced by Philip. Only Philip was directly called by Jesus.

3. *We must invite others to come and see Jesus.* Both Andrew and Philip went and told others (Simon and Nathanael, respectively) about Jesus and invited them to "come and see" (v. 46). Even though we cannot physically do this today, we can introduce others to Jesus through His bride, the church, or through Jesus' life and teaching in the Bible (see Heb. 4:12).

4. *The process can take time.* Even though Simon was introduced to Jesus by his brother Andrew, neither he nor Andrew left everything and followed Jesus until sometime later (see Matt. 4:18-20). Jesus taught that His disciples must count the cost of following Him (see Luke 14:25-33), and this process can take months, years, or even a lifetime.

Most of the disciples began following Jesus because of another person's testimony about Him. Think of someone in your life—such as a friend, a relative, a classmate, or a coworker—who does not know Jesus. What can you do to introduce that person to Jesus? How would you go about it?

What are a few questions you might ask them to start a conversation that leads to Christ? List as many as you can think of below.

Personal Study 2
Engaging with Others

From an evangelistic standpoint perhaps no conversation recorded in the Bible teaches us more about conversations that count than Jesus' conversation with a Samaritan woman, recorded in John 4:3-26,39-42. We will examine this passage in detail, analyzing it one segment at a time in order to draw out a number of important evangelistic principles.

PRINCIPLE 1: BE WILLING TO BREAK THROUGH SOCIAL AND CULTURAL BARRIERS. In John 4 we read the following about Jesus' movements and initial encounter with the Samaritan woman.

> [Jesus] left Judea and went back once more to Galilee. Now he had to go through Samaria. So he came to a town in Samaria called Sychar, near the plot of ground Jacob had given to his son Joseph. Jacob's well was there, and Jesus, tired as he was from the journey, sat down by the well. It was about noon. When a Samaritan woman came to draw water, Jesus said to her, "Will you give me a drink?" (His disciples had gone into the town to buy food.) The Samaritan woman said to him, "You are a Jew and I am a Samaritan woman. How can you ask me for a drink?" (For Jews do not associate with Samaritans.)
> **JOHN 4:3-9**

This encounter is instructive for at least three reasons.

1. There is some debate about whether Jesus actually "had" to go through Samaria (v. 4). The region of Samaria was located between Judea in the south and Galilee in the north. While going through Samaria was the quicked route, some Jews, due to their aversion to all things Samaritan, preferred to take the long way back to Galilee, thereby avoiding Samaria altogether. In contrast, Jesus was willing to cross over to "the wrong side of the tracks" as He went through life.
2. Jesus was not hostage to the prejudice, sexism, or racism of His day. Many Jews believed Samaritans to be an unclean "half-breed" because of their intermarriage with Assyrians during the exile.[1] Clearly, Jesus cared for none of this prejudice and was willing to engage in conversation with those whom His culture looked down on.

3. The woman herself was likely a social outcast, as evidenced by the fact that she came to the well alone at noon.[2] Jesus had every cultural reason to shun this woman, based on her ethnic identity, gender, and social status. She knew as much, hence her surprise when Jesus asked her for a drink. But Jesus did not overlook the *imago dei*—the image of God—that each person bears, and neither should we.

What social and cultural barriers are you afraid to cross, even to share the gospel?

PRINCIPLE 2: GENERATE CURIOSITY ABOUT JESUS. Having earned trust by violating social taboos, Jesus next piqued the Samaritan woman's curiosity.

> *Jesus answered her, "If you knew the gift of God and who it is that asks you for a drink, you would have asked him and he would have given you living water." "Sir," the woman said, "you have nothing to draw with and the well is deep. Where can you get this living water? Are you greater than our father Jacob, who gave us the well and drank from it himself, as did also his sons and his livestock?"*
> **JOHN 4:10-12**

Jesus used the well to start a conversation about Himself. By making the claim about living water, Jesus piqued the woman's curiosity. Even though the woman may not have believed Jesus right away, He certainly had her attention.

What is an example of something in our culture that you can use to begin a conversation about Jesus?

PRINCIPLE 3: PRESENT THE GOSPEL. Of course, the Samaritan woman was twice wrong. The "living water" (v. 10) Jesus offered didn't come from a well in the ground; Jesus was referring to the Holy Spirit, who gives eternal life (see John 7:38-39). Moreover, Jesus was far greater than the patriarchs (see Heb. 3:3). Still, Jesus had awakened her curiosity after making this audacious claim, and He followed it up with nothing less than the gospel message itself by offering her eternal life. John 4 records the following.

> *Jesus answered, "Everyone who drinks this water will be thirsty again, but whoever drinks the water I give them will never thirst. Indeed, the water I give them will become in them a spring of water welling up to eternal life." The woman said to him, "Sir, give me this water so that I won't get thirsty and have to keep coming here to draw water."*
>
> **JOHN 4:13-15**

Jesus' words are laden with meaning and echoes of Old Testament promises (see Isa. 12:3; 44:3; 49:10; 55:1-5; Jer. 2:13; Zech. 14:8). The woman was beginning to understand what Jesus was saying and the hope He offered.

Refer to your answer to the previous question. How can you bridge from that conversation starting point to the gospel?

PRINCIPLE 4: HIGHLIGHT THE NEED FOR THE GOSPEL. In response to the Samaritan woman's request, Jesus next turned to her sin. John 4 records the following.

> *He told her, "Go, call your husband and come back." "I have no husband," she replied. Jesus said to her, "You are right when you say you have no husband. The fact is, you have had five husbands, and the man you now have is not your husband. What you have just said is quite true."*
>
> **JOHN 4:16-18**

Jesus addressed the Samaritan woman's emotional needs for security and significance. Although these needs had driven her to a life of sexual immorality, Jesus invited her to come as she was so that God could satisfy the existential thirsts of her heart and soul.

What big questions are people asking that Jesus can answer? How do these questions help point the way to Jesus?

PRINCIPLE 5: WHEN OBJECTIONS ARISE, STAY FOCUSED ON WHAT MATTERS.
Jesus had tapped into an area of insecurity, a deep wound of guilt and hurt. The Samaritan woman naturally attempted to ward Him off from this area of her life. The next verses record:

> "Sir," the woman said, "I can see that you are a prophet. Our ancestors worshiped on this mountain [Mount Gerizim], but you Jews claim that the place where we must worship is in Jerusalem." "Woman," Jesus replied, "believe me, a time is coming when you will worship the Father neither on this mountain nor in Jerusalem. You Samaritans worship what you do not know; we worship what we do know, for salvation is from the Jews. Yet a time is coming and has now come when the true worshipers will worship the Father in the Spirit and in truth, for they are the kind of worshipers the Father seeks. God is spirit, and his worshipers must worship in the Spirit and in truth." The woman said, "I know that Messiah" (called Christ) "is coming. When he comes, he will explain everything to us." Then Jesus declared, "I, the one speaking to you—I am he."
> **JOHN 4:19-26**

The Samaritan woman raised no mere smokescreen. Around 388 BC the Samaritans had constructed a rival temple on Mount Gerizim that was later destroyed by John Hyrcanus, the Hasmonean ruler in Judea, in 128 BC.[3] This act caused a lasting rift between the two communities and explains much of the hostility between Jews and Samaritans. Therefore, it is not surprising that the woman's discovery that Jesus was a Jewish prophet prompted her to challenge Him by raising a major point of historical and theological contention.

How can we listen thoughtfully and attentively to objections without allowing ourselves to get sidetracked?

However, Jesus didn't take the bait. Instead, He focused on the three truths that really mattered.

1. *God's Word.* Because Samaritans rejected much of the Old Testament, they stood outside the stream of God's saving revelation. Jesus addressed the fact that the Samaritans worshiped a God they did not fully know. The integrity and authority of Scripture is never a place of compromise.
2. *Relationship with God.* Sidestepping the theological debate about the relative merits of Jerusalem and Mount Gerizim, Jesus instead focused on the person of God rather than a place. What mattered was not where someone worshiped but whom.
3. *The identity of Jesus.* Prior to His trial, Jesus' conversation with the Samaritan woman was His only open declaration that He was the Messiah. The disclosure of all who Jesus is—Messiah, Son of God, King, Prophet, Great High Priest—can be powerful when a heart is open to the truth.

This one conversation bore fruit for years to come. More immediately:

> *Many of the Samaritans from that town believed in [Jesus] because of the woman's testimony, "He told me everything I ever did." So when the Samaritans came to him, they urged him to stay with them, and he stayed two days. And because of his words many more became believers.*
>
> **JOHN 4:39-41**

Jesus not only lingered with the Samaritans for two days, but the testimony of the woman as a transformed insider also helped to persuade many people in Sychar. Later the ministry begun there paved the way for successful evangelism by Philip (see Acts 8:4-13), followed by Peter and John (see vv. 14-25).

In their book *I Once Was Lost* authors Don Everts and Doug Schaupp outline five thresholds that people generally pass through on their journeys to becoming followers of Jesus:

1. Trusting a Christian
2. Becoming curious about Jesus
3. Opening up to change
4. Seeking God
5. Entering the kingdom[4]

Consider these thresholds as you answer the following questions.

Think of the social networks in which you are an insider. At which of the five thresholds would you place each of the main people in your life?

How can you use questions and stories in ways that provoke curiosity about Jesus?

Why might you need to gently but boldly call people out of fear and complacency?

Paul instructs us to be both wise and gracious (see Col. 4:5-6). What does it mean for speech to be gracious? What does it mean for our words to be seasoned with salt?

How does this manner of speech affect the way you answer each person?

For further study read the articles on pages 148–51.

QUESTIONS THAT COUNT

Every week we have dozens of conversations with people where we live, work, and play. Many of those conversations never go beyond small talk. Yet each conversation presents an opportunity for you to know someone on a deeper level. The following questions are designed to lead your conversations beyond the surface level directly to the heart. Asking these types of questions and actively listening to the answers are great ways to begin conversations that lead to the gospel.

Use these questions to start conversations with nonbelieving friends.

What was the best part of your week?
What was the worst part of your week?

What has been on your mind most recently?

When was the happiest time in your life?
Why?

What are you good at?

What are your dreams for the future?

If money were not an issue and you could do
anything you wanted, what would you do?
Why?

What were you like as a child? Do you think
you are different now? In what ways?

What is your best childhood memory?

What family member are you most alike?
What family member are you most different
from? In what ways?

To which family member are you closest?
Are you close to your other family members?

Who is your best friend, and what is his or
her best quality?

How would your best friends describe you?

Who has had the most significant influence on
your life? Why?

What would you change about yourself if you
could change one thing?

Did you grow up in a religious home?
Would you raise your children the same way?
Why or why not?

What do you find most frustrating about
religion?

If you could make one law, what would it be?
If you could break one law, what would it be?

In one word, what do you think is the most
important trait for a leader to have?

What causes 80 percent of your stress?

Have you ever had an experience that made
you think God might exist?

SUPPLEMENTAL ARTICLES

WEEK 1 ARTICLES

The Apologist's First Question
Ravi Zacharias

I have little doubt that the single greatest obstacle to the impact of the gospel has not been its inability to provide answers but the failure on the part of Christians to live it out. I remember well in the early days of my Christian faith talking to a close Hindu friend. He was questioning the experience of conversion as being supernatural. He absolutely insisted that conversion was nothing more than a decision to lead a more ethical life and that, in most cases, it was not any different from other ethical religions. I had heard his argument before.

But then he said something I have never forgotten: "If this conversion is truly supernatural, why isn't it more evident in the lives of so many Christians I know?" His question is a troublesome one. In fact, it is so deeply disturbing a question that I think of all the challenges to belief, this is the most difficult question of all. I have never struggled with my own personal faith as far as intellectual challenges to the gospel are concerned. But I have often had struggles of the soul in trying to figure out why the Christian faith is not more visible.

After lecturing at a major American university, I was driven to the airport by the organizer of the event. I was quite jolted by what he told me. He said, "My wife brought our neighbor last night. She's a medical doctor and hadn't been to anything like this before. On their way home my wife asked her what she thought of it all." He paused and then continued, "Do you know what she said?" Rather reluctantly, I shook my head. "She said, 'That was a very powerful evening. The arguments were very persuasive. I wonder what he's like in his private life.' "

Because my Hindu friend had not witnessed spiritual transformation in the life of Christians, whatever answers he received were nullified. In the doctor's case the answers were intellectually and existentially satisfying, but she still needed to know whether they really made a difference in the life of the one proclaiming them. The Irish evangelist Gypsy Smith once said, "There are five Gospels. Matthew, Mark, Luke, John, and the Christian, and some people will never read the first four." In other words, the message is seen before it is heard. For both the Hindu questioner and the American doctor, the answers to their questions were not enough; they depended on the visible transformation of the person offering them.

First Peter 3:15 offers the defining statement:

> *In your hearts revere Christ as Lord. Always be prepared to give an answer* [apologia] *to everyone who asks you to give the reason for the hope that you have. But do this with gentleness and respect.*
> **1 PETER 3:15**

Notice that before the answer is given, the person giving the answer is called to a certain prerequisite. The lordship of Christ over the life of the apologist is foundational to all answers given. Peter, of all the disciples, knew well how to ask questions and also how fickle the human heart is. He knew the seductive power of the spectacular in momentary enthrallment. He knew what it was to betray someone and to fail. He knew what it was to try to explain the gospel, as he did at Pentecost. Peter's strong reminder of the heart of the apologist is the basis of all apologetic attempts.

With character in mind, there follow two immediate imperatives: the quality of life lived and the clarity of answers given. The way a Christian's life is lived will determine the impact on believers and skeptics alike. This is a defining line because the claim by the believer is unique. The claim is that of a new birth in Christ. After all, no Buddhists or Hindus or Muslims claim their lives of devotion to be supernatural, yet they often live more consistent lives. And how often does a so-called Christian, even while teaching some of the loftiest truths someone could ever teach, live a life bereft of that beauty and character? In apologetics the question is often asked, If there is only one way, how is it that there are few in all of creation who qualify? That question is actually more potent than the questioner realizes. It should further be raised, Out of the few who actually qualify, why are even fewer living it out?

When Jesus spoke to the woman at the well (see John 4:1-26), she raised one question after another as if that were really her problem. It would have been very easy for the Lord to call her bluff with some castigating words. Instead, like a gentle and nimble-handed goldsmith, he rubbed away the markings of sin and pain in her life until she was amazed at how much true gold he brought out in her. He gave her hope, knowing all along who she was on the inside. Jesus was clear: the value of the person is an essential part of the message.

Every Christian ought to take time to reflect seriously on the question, Has God truly wrought a miracle in my life? Is my own heart proof of the supernatural intervention of God? That is the apologist's first question.[1]

The Most Difficult Questions
Ravi Zacharias

Out of the scores of letters I have received over the years, one in particular stands out. The writer asked, "Why has God made it so difficult to believe in Him? If I loved somebody and had infinite power, I would use that power to show myself more obviously. Why has God made it so difficult to see His presence and His plan?" It is a powerful question that is both felt and intellectual at the same time. Someone might ask, "Why is God so hidden?" The question ultimately gains momentum and parks itself in our heart's genuine search for meaning, belonging, and relationship with our Creator.

I recall the restlessness and turning point in my own life. I had come to believe that life had no meaning. Nothing seemed to connect. When still in my teens, I found myself lying in a hospital bed after an attempted suicide. The struggle for answers when met by despair led me along that tragic path. But there in my hospital room the Scriptures were brought and read to me. For the first time I engaged the direct answers of God with my seeking heart. The profound realization of the news that God could be personally known drew me, with sincerity and determination, to plumb the depths of that claim. With a simple prayer of trust in that moment, the change from a desperate heart to one that found the fullness of meaning became a reality for me.

An immediate change came in my perception of God's handiwork in ways I had never seen before. The marvel of discovering splendor in the ordinary was the work of God in my heart. Over a period of time, I was able to study, pursue, and understand how to respond to more intricate questions of the mind.

That divine encounter of coming to know God brought meaning to my life and made answers reachable. I believe God intervenes in each of our lives. He speaks to us in different ways and at different times so that we can know it is He who is the author of our very personality, that His answers are both propositional and relational (and sometimes in reverse order), and that His presence stills the storms of the heart.

Oddly enough, in history the most questioning and resistant people became God's mouthpieces to skeptics. Consider Peter, Paul, and Thomas, just to name a few. They questioned, they wrestled, they challenged. But once convinced, they spoke and wrote and persuaded people in the most stubborn of circumstances. That is why they willingly paid the ultimate price, even as they sought God's power and presence in those dark nights of the soul.

In the end, in the face of difficult questions, the answers that are given and received must be both felt and real, with the firm knowledge that God is nearer than we might think. Yes, the Scriptures reveal, as many can attest, that this assurance of nearness sometimes comes at a cost, like any relationship of love and commitment. But God is grander than any wondrous sight we may behold and the answer to every heart's deepest question. The final consummation of that glimpse is yet future. I firmly believe, as the apostle Paul declared:

> *Things which eye has not seen and ear has not heard,*
> *And which have not entered the heart of man,*
> *All that God has prepared for those who love Him.*
> **1 CORINTHIANS 2:9, NASB**

Then we shall see, not darkly but face-to-face. That is when the soul will feel the ultimate touch, and the silence will be one of knowing with awesome wonder. The only thing we would want hidden is how blind we were.

WEEK 2 ARTICLES

Everyone Believes in a Virgin Birth
Vince Vitale

In correspondence with an old friend, a retired Princeton University professor, he detailed his objections to the Christian faith. His final remark seemed to overshadow all other considerations and was authoritatively written as if to definitively close the argument: "Nor can I believe in a virgin birth." Such a belief was apparently implausible, absurd, immature.

Why is the virgin birth often the most problematic miracle to accept? Why is it more troubling than the thought of Jesus walking on water? Or multiplying the loaves? Perhaps because we are content to let God do as He pleases with His own body, and we are delighted to be the recipient of gifts. However, we are offended by the thought of a miracle that inconveniences us, that has the potential to disrupt our plans and preferences.

I considered responding to my friend with positive reasons for believing in the virgin birth, but then I realized that he was, in fact, already committed to a virgin birth.

We find one virgin birth in the Christmas story:

> *"How will this be," Mary asked the angel, "since I am a*
> *virgin?" The angel answered, "The Holy Spirit will come on*
> *you, and the power of the Most High will overshadow you.*
> *So the holy one to be born will be called the Son of God."*
> **LUKE 1:34-35**

Admittedly, this event is out of the ordinary. But criticism without alternative is empty; a hypothesis is only plausible or implausible relative to the alternative hypotheses that present themselves. So what exactly is the alternative?

My colleague Professor John Lennox once debated another Princeton professor, Peter Singer, one of the world's most influential atheists. Lennox challenged him to answer this question: "Why are we here?" This was Professor Singer's response:

> *We can assume that somehow in the primeval soup we got*
> *collections of molecules that became self-replicating; and I*
> *don't think we need any miraculous or mysterious [explanation].[1]*

The idea of self-replicating molecules somehow emerging from a primeval soup strikes me as leaving substantial room for mystery. In fact, without further clarification this theory sounds similar to a virgin birth.

Or take Cambridge physicist Stephen Hawking's attempt to propose an atheistic explanation for our universe:

> *The universe can and will create itself from nothing.*
> *Spontaneous creation is the reason there is something*
> *rather than nothing, why the universe exists, why we exist.*[2]

But physical matter doesn't normally materialize from nothing, so this account also presents itself as outside the realm of the ordinary. Is this a less miraculous birth than the Christmas story?

Or finally, consider the position of the prominent atheist philosopher Quentin Smith:

> *The fact of the matter is that the most reasonable belief is that we*
> *came from nothing, by nothing and for nothing. ... We should ...*
> *acknowledge our foundation in nothingness and feel awe at the marvelous*
> *fact that we have a chance to participate briefly in this incredible*
> *sunburst that interrupts without reason the reign of non-being.*[3]

That is a refreshingly honest characterization, but again, it is not at all clear why a foundation in nothingness should be viewed as comparatively more reasonable than a foundation in God.

The fact is, we live in a miraculous world. Regardless of a person's worldview, the extraordinariness of the universe is evident to theists, atheists, and agnostics alike. It is therefore not a matter of whether we believe in a virgin birth but which virgin birth we choose to accept. We can believe in the virgin birth of an atheistic universe that is indifferent to us—a universe where "there is, at bottom, no design, no purpose, no evil and no good, nothing but blind pitiless indifference."[4] Alternatively, we can believe in the virgin birth of a God who loves us so deeply that He "became flesh and made his dwelling among us" (John 1:14). Immanuel, God with us.

Jesus was born in fragility like the rest of us. The night before He died, He spoke words that resonate with anyone who has known despair: "My soul is over-whelmed with sorrow to the point of death" (Mark 14:34). Between birth and death Jesus knew the experience of weeping at a dear friend's tomb (see John 11:35);

He also knew the isolation of having friends desert Him and flee when He needed them most (see Mark 14:50).

Depth of relationship is possible only between people who have been through the worst together. Because of Jesus—because the One who birthed the universe was also born among us—that depth of relationship is possible with God. That is what we celebrate at Christmas.

When I was growing up near New York City, one of my most vivid childhood memories of Christmas is of homeless people begging on street corners. I would give some change if I had it, but imagine someone who offered to trade His home for a cold street corner, who, instead of giving a few coins, handed over the keys to His house. Imagine someone who, being in very nature God, did not consider equality with God something to be used to his own advantage (see Phil. 2:6-7).

In Jesus, God literally came and lived in our home—with all of its suffering and mess and shame—and He offered us the home that it will one day be: an eternal home where "[God] will wipe every tear from [our] eyes," where there will be "no more death or mourning or crying or pain" (Rev. 21:4). Or, as Tolkien puts it, where "everything sad [is] going to come untrue."[5]

Has Science Disproved God?
Vince Vitale

The first time I met people who encouraged me to consider God, I was in college. I began by reading the Gospels, and I found myself attracted to the Christian message. I was especially attracted to the person of Jesus and the beautiful life He lived. But to be honest, I assumed that belief in God was for people who didn't think hard enough. I assumed that smart people somewhere had already disproved belief in God. More specifically, I assumed that there was some purely scientific way of understanding the world and that miracles had no part in it.

I remember picking up a book in a university bookshop around that time and reading the back cover, which summarized the book as an attempt to hold on to a form of Christianity while explaining away all the supposed miracles of Jesus in scientific terms. And I remember hoping it could be done, because I was longing for the person of Jesus, but I thought the traditional account of Christianity was just too extraordinary to believe. I assumed that the burden of proof for belief in God must be higher because God is such an extraordinary option.

Richard Dawkins puts it this way:

> If you want to believe in … unicorns, or tooth fairies, Thor or Yahweh—the onus is on you to say why you believe in it. The onus is not on the rest of us to say why we do not.[1]

I bought into that way of thinking—that God is the crazy option, whereas a fully naturalistic and fully scientifically explainable universe is the sober, sensible, rational option. Without ever reasoning it through, I accepted the cultural myth that we used to need God to miraculously explain thunder and lightning, rainbows and shooting stars. But now that we have scientific explanations for these things, we should stop believing in God.

That is actually not a very good argument. A good engineer does not need to keep stepping in to override systems and fix malfunctions. If God is a good engineer, isn't the ability to explain His design in terms of consistently functioning processes exactly what we should expect?

Moreover, we no longer think we need the moon to explain lunacy. *(Lunacy* comes from the word *lunar* because people used to think the position of the moon explained madness.) Does that mean we should no longer believe in the moon? Should we become not only a-theists but a-moonists?[2] Of course not. Even if the moon doesn't explain madness, there are many other things, such as ocean tides, that it does explain. Likewise, the reasons for believing in God extend far beyond scientific reasons and include historical, philosophical, moral, aesthetic, experiential, and relational reasons.

Without thinking it through, I jumped from science to scientism—from the fact that science can explain a lot to the assumption that it can explain everything. However, just because the advancement of science has taught us new things about the way the universe works, that doesn't tell us whether there is a who behind the how.

A computer expert can provide a full scientific explanation of the way Microsoft Office works. But that would not prove that Bill Gates does not exist; it would not prove that there is no who behind the how. To the contrary, it would show that Bill Gates is really smart!

The how question (a question of mechanism) does not answer the who question (a question of agency), and it also does not answer the why question (a question of purpose): Why was Microsoft Office created? We can get an answer to that question only if Bill Gates chooses to share it with us—if the creator of the system chooses to reveal it.

Some of the standard arguments against God based on science are actually not very strong. But I think there are a lot of people out there like I was. People who might be open to Christian faith but who have assumed that science has made that impossible. They have bought into a cultural myth about the battle between science and religion without actually thinking it through.

I am so thankful that I met some friends many years ago who communicated to me in an accessible way their reasons for God, including their reasons for thinking science and God are in no way incompatible. I found myself persuaded. In fact, today I would agree with Peter van Inwagen, one of the world's foremost philosophers, when he says, "No discovery of science (so far, at any rate) has the least tendency to show that there is no God."[3]

I would actually go further. Not only do I think science is in no way incompatible with belief in God, but I also think science points strongly to the existence of God. There are four reasons I believe this.

1. *The universe has a beginning.*
2. *The universe is knowable.*
3. *The universe is regular.*
4. *The universe is finely tuned for life.*

I believe all four of these facts about our universe are best explained by the existence of God.

WEEK 3 ARTICLES

A Kaleidoscope of Colors
Ravi Zacharias

When our son was only four years old and we moved to a different city, he raised a question that brought rounds of laughter from the whole family and even prompted a wistful thought. Riding in the car one day, right out of the blue he turned to my wife (who is from Canada) and said, "Mummy, when do we turn black?" Caught completely off guard, she said, "I don't know what you mean." "Well," sounded the pensive, albeit innocent, childish voice, "You are white, we are beige, and Daddy is brown. When do we turn black?"

How nice it would be if life provided such a sequence of colors! In his young mind, magnificently untainted by years of biases and indoctrination, he saw life as a time-released kaleidoscope of colors and apparently envisioned the possibility of each of us experiencing the joys and hurts of all. How much more understanding of one another we would be if each of us could live for a time in another person's world and be subsumed in someone else's life story!

The multiplicity of ethnicities offers many delights; how intriguing are the various cuisines, traditions, art, accents, and literature of our world. In the West globalization has brought the riches of pluralization to our neighborhoods and smartphones. As one speaker I heard once quipped, "Where else but in Los Angeles [or, I might add, Toronto or London] would you find a fast-food stand where a Korean is selling kosher tacos?"

Yet with pluralization has come pluralism, the phenomenon or process by which all ideas and worldviews have become accepted as equally valid and true. Naturalism, Christianity, Hinduism, Islam—choose whatever you wish because all narratives lead to the same conclusion and essentially teach the same things. That is what is implied. But do they?

I was once asked by a student from Nepal studying in an American university, "Why Christianity?" In other words, with the numerous religions in the world, what's so distinct about Christianity? I have been asked this question countless times around the globe, and I am fascinated by the fact that the Christian faith is the only one that is ever raised.

Answering such a question demands serious sensitivity. You see, religious pluralism is a belief system that sounds good but does disservice to all religions. All religions are exclusive. That is a fact. If they were not, they would not be making any truth claims. Indeed, it is the very nature of truth that presents us with this reality. Truth by definition is exclusive. Every proposition and assertion in contradictory worldviews cannot be true. If every assertion and claim were true, then there would really be no distinctive claim, in effect making all religions equally true or false. Truth has two edges to its claims. Someone cannot claim mutually exclusive beliefs.

The reality is that even those who deny the exclusivity of truth, in effect, exclude those who do not deny it. The truth quickly emerges. The law of noncontradiction applies to reality: two contradictory statements cannot both be true in the same sense. Thus, to deny the law of noncontradiction is to affirm it at the same time. You may as well talk about a one-ended stick as talk about truth being all-inclusive.

Furthermore, every religion has its starting points and its deductions, and those starting points exclude counterperspectives. For example, Hinduism has two nonnegotiable beliefs: karma and reincarnation. No Hindu will trade these away. Buddhism denies the essential notion of the self. Buddhists believe that the self, as we understand it, does not exist, and our ceasing to desire will result in the end of all suffering. If we deny these premises, we deny Buddhism.

Islam believes that Mohammad is the last and final prophet and that the Qur'an is the perfect revelation. If we deny those two premises, we have denied Islam. Even naturalism, which poses as irreligion, is exclusive. Naturalism teaches that anything supernatural or metaphysical is outside the realm of evidence and purely an opinion, not a matter of fact.

In the Christian faith we believe Jesus is the consummate expression of God in the person of His Son and is the Savior and Redeemer of the world. We cannot deny these premises and continue to be Christians.

All religions are not the same. All religions do not point to God. All religions do not say that all religions are the same. At the heart of every religion is an uncompromising commitment to a particular way of defining who God is or is not and, accordingly, of defining life's purpose.

So the question is not, Which of these religions is all-encompassing? Rather, it is, Which one of these religions will we deny as being reasonable and consistent? Which one of these will we be able to sustain by argument and by evidence? We can have pluralism in cuisine, clothing styles, accents, and a kaleidoscope of other things. But if pluralism means ideational relativism and the destruction of the law of noncontradiction, it is incoherent and ultimately unlivable.

I think, for instance, of one of my closest Hindu friends who struggled for years with whether the teachings of his religion were truly livable, particularly the doctrine of karma. He was sitting in my living room when he spoke out loud: "If every birth is a rebirth and every birth is the consequence of previous karmic practices, what was I paying for in my first birth? I cannot have an infinite series of rebirths, or I would not be in this birth. Therefore I must have had a first birth. What was I paying for then?"

I just stared at him and said, "You have to answer that question."

He said it simply did not make sense. He had to have a first birth and ever since then was in karmic deficit. He said, "If I go to the bank, every bank manager will tell me what my indebtedness is and how long I have to pay it off. What sort of system is life itself, in which I have no clue about what I owe and how many births it will take for me to pay it back?"

Those unanswerable questions sent my friend on a pursuit of truth, and he finally found grace and forgiveness in Jesus.

Likewise, part of my response to the Nepalese student who asked me about Christianity was to share with him that only in Jesus could he find the answers to the deepest questions of the soul, answers that correspond to reality and in totality are systemically coherent. Indeed, only Jesus describes our condition, provides for our malady, explains suffering, offers His life as an atoning sacrifice, and rose again from the dead to give eternal life to all who would believe. The gospel is the only story in which grace and forgiveness are central and unearned—and that is good news to all people everywhere, whatever color or ethnicity.

That is why Jesus made the astounding statement "Everyone on the side of truth listens to me" (John 18:37). All religions may have hints of truth and aspects of goodness. But only in Jesus Christ do we see the consummate expression of the true, the good, and the beautiful. In Him was the embodiment of grace and truth. The disciples rightly said to Him, "Lord, to whom shall we go? You have the words of eternal life" (John 6:68).

Jesus tasted death for all of us, whatever our race or creed. He gives life to all who come to Him. Heaven is the ultimate equalizer and the place of perpetual novelty.[1]

The Trajectory of Truth
Vince Vitale

We live in a posttruth society. That's what *The Economist* claimed at the close of 2016, when the Oxford English Dictionary chose posttruth as its word of the year. Go back a bit further, and having 11 percent of America believe that you are honest and trustworthy was good enough to have a 9 percent lead in the race to be the next president of the United States. But of course, even the polls were posttrue.

We are very confused about the truth. There's the truth, and then there's the naked truth. There's the truth, and then there's the gospel truth (though the gospel is taken to be obviously false). There's the honest truth, and then there's the God's honest truth (but that has nothing to do with God).

We stretch the truth and bend the truth and twist the truth. We bury the truth because the truth hurts. When we want something to be false, we knock on wood. When we want something to be true, we cross our fingers. Which wooden cross are we trusting in?

Why do we have such a confused relationship with the truth? Fear. We're afraid of truth. Truth has so often been abused that experience has taught us the trajectory of truth—the trajectory of believing you are right and others are wrong—is from truth to disagreement to devaluing to intolerance to extremism to violence to terrorism.

And if that is the trajectory, then the people who are committed to truth are in fact terrorists in the making. If that is the trajectory, then truth is an act of war, and an act of war leaves you with only two options: fight or flee.

Much of Western society is fleeing. Everything around us is structured to avoid disagreement about the truth. We spend most of our time on Facebook and Twitter, where we can like and retweet, but there is no option to dislike. Sports no longer teach us how to disagree. In professional sports we replay every call to avoid disagreement. In youth sports we don't keep score, and everyone gets a trophy.

When it comes to dating, we use online sites that match us with someone so similar in beliefs, background, and personality that as much disagreement as possible is avoided. We no longer meet people different from us at coffee shops because we go to the Starbucks drive-through. We no longer meet people while asking for directions because we just search online. We no longer meet people while shopping because everything we could ever need or want is delivered to our door. Culturally, everything around us is set up to avoid disagreement.

The alternative to fleeing is fighting. I was walking around Oxford University, and two guys walking just ahead of me were having a spirited conversation about how crazy they found certain Christian positions on ethical issues. One of them wondered out loud whether the only solution would be to shame Christians out of their positions.

His friend quickly responded, "Yeah, that's what we should do! We should ridicule them mercilessly in the most insensitive ways we can think of." That is an exact quote. Then they both made a right turn and swiped their faculty cards to enter the theoretical-physics building.

These were probably scholars at Oxford, a place that prides itself on intellectual freedom and the exchange of ideas, and merciless, insensitive ridicule was the best strategy they could offer to resolve disagreement. I found myself wondering how many of the beliefs they hold in theoretical physics will one day be considered ridiculous.

How do people get to this point? How does someone get to the point at which merciless ridicule seems like the best way forward?

I think it's because some people have come to see truth as more important than love. If truth is greater than love, then you fight; then the end goal of truth justifies whatever means necessary, whether the means of haughty academics or the means of ISIS. If truth is greater than love, then love is a temptation—a distraction threatening to avert our attention from what is truly important. If truth is greater than love, then those who disagree with us are enemies, and warmth toward our enemies must be extinguished in favor of the cold, hard facts.

The alternative is that love is greater than truth. Then you flee. You flee from the dangers of truth and adopt a pluralism that assures us, "All truths are equally valid." Does that include the claim that all truth claims are not equally valid? One college student told my colleague, Abdu Murray, that he does not believe it is his place to disagree with anyone.

Abdu said, "Sure you do."

The student said, "No, I don't."

Abdu said, "You just did."

Philosophically, that is how quickly pluralism runs into incoherence. But if truth starts a person down a path that ends in extremism, violence, and terrorism, then philosophical incoherence might seem like a price worth paying.

Either truth is greater than love, or love is greater than truth. Fight or flee. This is the cultural ultimatum we are living in. What is your choice?

Maybe there is another way. Jesus disagreed with us. His very coming was an act of disagreement with us—a statement that we require saving because our lives have disagreed so badly with what God intended for us.

Jesus' loving sacrifice for us was the very content of His disagreement; it was His very statement that we are sinners in need of a Savior. God cut the link between disagreement and devaluing by making His communication of truth one with and the same as His communication of love.

Not "Truth is greater than love." Not "Love is greater than truth." "God is love" (1 John 4:8), and God is truth (see John 14:6). And therefore, love is truth.

Only in Jesus does truth equal love, and therefore only Jesus can get us out of the cultural ultimatum we are stuck in: fight or flee. Every other worldview makes a choice between love and truth. Jesus refused to, because in Him and only in Him, love and truth are one and the same.

So the next time we have a choice between love and truth, let's refuse to choose. Instead, let's remember when the Truth—Jesus Himself—was stretched. Let's remember when the Truth was twisted and bent, when the Truth was naked. Let's remember when the Truth hurt and when the Truth was buried—and ultimately triumphed.

Let's remember which wooden cross we are trusting in. And let's remember that love that is not truth is not love, and truth that is not love is not truth.

WEEK 4 ARTICLES

Moral Injunctions about Morality
Ravi Zacharias

"Let any one of you who is without sin be the first to throw a stone" (John 8:7). We often hear this thought posited as a rationale for casting aside any type of public moralizing. Evidently, society cannot completely shake off its bequest from a Christian worldview. Ironically, this moral conviction is given even as we are stridently reminded that all morality is a private matter and not for public enforcement. But if all moral convictions are a private matter, why is this conviction not kept private too? Why is it publicly enjoined?

Interestingly, in every instance when I have asked people who cite this verse if they are aware of the context in which those words were uttered, virtually none could identify it. One said it related to the woman caught in adultery. I followed up and asked if he was aware of what prompted that imperative and to whom Jesus had said those words. There was silence. Significantly, the entire confrontation came about because the Pharisees were seeking to trap Jesus into either explicitly defending the law of Moses or implicitly overruling it. The whole scenario was a ploy not to reveal the truth of a moral law but to trap Jesus.

Fascinatingly, Jesus exposed the Pharisees' spiritual bankruptcy by showing them that at the heart of law is God's character. A spiritual essence precedes moral injunctions. Many people who vociferously demand that only the one without sin may cast the first stone would not grant credence to God's Word in its numerous other pronouncements. And for some people, sin is not even a viable concept. This selective use of Scripture is the very game Jesus' questioners were playing. But what is lawful can withstand the test of human guile only if it reflects an understanding of what is sinful. Sin by definition points to an absolute moral lawgiver. When the law is quoted while the reality of sin is denied, self-aggrandizing motives can override character. Thus, in our spiritually amputated world the art of obscuring truth has become a science in courtroom and political theatrics.

Herein lies what I believe is the crucial death of our times. There is no transcendent context within which to discuss moral theory. Just as words, in order to have meaning, must point beyond themselves to a commonly understood, real existence, so also must reality point beyond itself to commonly accepted essence. Otherwise, reality has no moral quotient whatsoever, and moral meaning dissolves into the subjective, rendering it beyond debate. Only the transcendent can unchangingly provide fixed moral worth.

But this death of the transcendent comes with a two-edged sword, both for the skeptic and the Christian alike. Yes, the law has moral value but not as a means for shrewd lawyers to play deadly word games, minimize immorality, and kill the truth. At the same time, the law has spiritual value so that we do not destroy the truly repentant individual. The grace of God abounds to the worst in our midst. Hidden in the odious nature of our failures is the scandalous secret of God's forgiveness. When the prodigal returned in Luke 15, the anger he faced was not the father's but the older son's, who failed to understand how marvelous was the grace of his father. Throughout history God's way of dealing with the reckless has disclosed how dramatic are His ways. We must allow for such possibilities. "This son of mine was dead and is alive again" (v. 24). Death lay in the wanderings of the passions and the seriousness of wrongdoing. Life was spelled in true repentance to return and "sin no more" (John 8:11, NASB). But let's take note. Forgiveness does not minimize the wrongdoing. It is offered in full recognition of the heinousness of what is being forgiven.

On the contrary, when words, consequences, purity, and transcendent contexts have died, a pigsty awaits. Only if we remember our Father's address can we know where to return for forgiveness and love. But if we insist on arguing as quick-witted political powermongers or legal wordsmiths with no spiritual context, we may kill both law and love. That, I am afraid, is the abyss over which we often hover.

Yet I am confident that as precipitous as the edge seems, God has always been in the business of rescue. The truth is that as human beings, we all fall short. Our only hope is for an understanding of God's ways, through which forgiveness and responsibility come in balance. There is indeed another bridge, one on which a body was broken so that a path was made that we might cross over and live. In that cross lie both judgment and mercy. The Maker of all the earth cannot be fooled by shades of meaning, nor can He be obliterated by the shadows of death. James Russell Lowell closed his hymn "Once to Every Man and Nation" with these words:

> *Tho' the cause of evil prosper,*
> *Yet the truth alone is strong;*
> *Tho' her portion be the scaffold,*
> *And upon the throne be wrong:*
> *Yet that scaffold sways the future,*
> *And, behind the dim unknown,*
> *Standeth God within the shadow,*
> *Keeping watch above His own.*[1]

God is our help in ages past and our only hope for years to come.

On Being Human
Ravi Zacharias

With the arrival of cloning, the Human Genome Project, and advances in artificial intelligence, the nature of what it means to be a person becomes increasingly urgent. All bioethical questions ultimately require a concept of human essence as their point of reference.

Consider the Internet egg auction in which people could place bids on the chromosomes of eight female models. The website promoter hailed the spectacle as "Darwin's natural selection at its very best." Now many of us might react with visceral repulsion, but the site nonetheless generated hundreds of thousands of hits within the first few days of the auction.[1]

Commentator Brent Waters wrote:

> Although the auction was greeted generally with disgust,
> it is interesting to note the most prominent objection raised
> against it was that it was tantamount to consumer fraud.
> Successful bidders might not obtain the attractive children
> they were imagining. As various commentators explained,
> even if these eggs were joined with the "best" ... there was
> no guarantee of a "perfect" baby. All sorts of things could go
> wrong, resulting in a very disappointing child, because each
> roll of the genetic dice cannot be predicted in advance.[2]

Astounding! The decision to have a child is reduced to the economic return on a bid and whether the child would be sufficiently attractive not to be a disappointment. Is there not more to being human?

Think of it this way. If a computer could be programmed so thoroughly with the strategies involved in chess that it could defeat our brightest champion, would we then say that this computer is more human than the world's greatest chess player? Not likely, for to do so would reduce intelligence to computational efficiency, memory, and physical components.

In contrast, personhood, according to the Christian understanding, cannot be reduced to form or function. Indeed, our identity is sacred by definition, for we have been created by God to bear His image. We have been endowed with a moral nature, with the capacity to give love and understand goodness. A child, then, does not find her worth in physical beauty or mental prowess but in reflecting the beauty of her Creator. There is a transcendent value in being human, rooted in the very being of God.

As we wade our way through the morass of bioethics, we must not look at the face and intelligence quotient of a human but instead at the face and mind of God. Only then can we truly understand what it means to be human.

WEEK 5 ARTICLES

Whatever Makes You Happy
Vince Vitale

Imagine there were a machine that would give you any experience you desired (maybe before long there will be!). You could choose to experience winning Olympic gold, falling in love, or making a great scientific discovery, and the neurons in your brain would be stimulated in such a way that you would experience a simulation of actually doing these things. Although in reality you would be floating in a tank of goo with electrodes hooked up to your brain, you would be experiencing total pleasure. Given the choice, should you preprogram your experiences and plug into this machine for the rest of your life?[1]

I join philosopher Robert Nozick, who first devised this thought experiment in the 1970s, in thinking we should not plug into this experience machine. His reluctance suggests the falsity of hedonism, a view dating back over two millennia to the Greek philosophers Democritus and Epicurus. If all that mattered were pleasure (in other words, if hedonism were true), we should plug into the experience machine, and we should encourage everyone we know to plug in as well.

In reality, however, we rightly care about more than just happiness or pleasure. We not only want to feel loved; we want to actually be loved. We not only want to dream of accomplishing our dreams; we want to actually accomplish them. We not only want to feel inside as if we have made a difference in life; we want to actually make a difference. Hedonism is not the desire of our hearts; it is all that is left when every other "ism" has failed us.

One academic book suggested that, based on hedonistic assumptions, because some animals can feel pleasure like people but cannot suffer in some of the worst ways as people can, those animals could be understood to be more valuable than humans.[2] If the acquisition of pleasure and the avoidance of pain are the measure of all, these animals score well on pleasure, with fewer deductions for the complex psychological pains such as anxiety and disappointment to which the human psyche is vulnerable. This same assumption led utilitarian Jeremy Bentham to the view that "the game of push-pin [a children's game] is of equal value with the arts and sciences of music and poetry."[3] The problem here is not with the logic leading to the conclusions but with the underlying assumption that pleasure is the sole determinant of value.

Pleasure and happiness are good things, but they are not the only good things. We should care not only about feeling good on the inside but also about truth and about the impact our lives have beyond ourselves. As C. S. Lewis put it, if happiness were all he was after, a good bottle of port would do the trick.[4]

People frequently tell me they don't need God in their lives because "I'm happy as I am." That's great! I believe happiness is a gift from the God who "fills your hearts with joy" (Acts 14:17). But Christianity offers so much more than happiness. The person in the experience machine is very happy as they are. Some animals may be very happy as they are. Should we therefore plug into the experience machine or wish we were animals? In either case the result of hedonism is the loss of humanity.

According to Christianity, there was one person in history who could have plugged into the experience machine: Jesus. In fact, Jesus could have done one better. He could have refrained from creating the material universe at all and simply enjoyed the perfect pleasure of relationship within the Trinity for all eternity. Or, once He had created, He could have stayed far away from the vulnerabilities of this world. He could have lived a nonhuman existence overflowing with pleasure and devoid of all pain.

Instead, Jesus created a world that would be broken by His creatures—a world that would grieve Him in many respects—and He chose to enter that world as a human being, with all the susceptibilities to pain and suffering that human existence guarantees. This is the life Jesus chose. As He put it, "No one takes [my life] from me, but I lay it down of my own accord" (John 10:18). In choosing this life over infinite, uninterrupted pleasure yet living the most universally lauded life of all time, Jesus displayed a powerful, sustained argument against hedonism.

A few years ago I saw a commercial that depicted a baby being born, and then in thirty seconds it fast-forwarded through the child's entire life until he was old, gray, and hunched over, finally falling down and crashing into a grave. Then these words flashed across the screen: "Life is short. Play more Xbox." Really? Is that the best we have got? Life is short, and it is fragile. Is the answer really just to play more Xbox—to distract ourselves and try not to think about it, to plug into an Xbox experience machine because we can do nothing about the human condition? The future the Bible offers is very different:

> *God's dwelling place is now among the people, and he will dwell with them.*
> *They will be his people, and God himself will be with them and be their God.*
> *"He will wipe every tear from their eyes. There will be no more death"*
> *or mourning or crying or pain, for the old order of things has passed away.*
>
> **REVELATION 21:3-4**

Let's hope with those for whom hedonism is not an option. Let's hope with them that death need not be our end. Let's hope that God is with each person, until the very end, offering this hope.

Hedonism fails, and we know it fails. It fails regardless of whether we pursue pleasure or are denied the pursuit of pleasure. Yet if we are brave enough to consider the questions and answer them honestly, how much of our lives is lived worshiping at the altar of pleasure? What percentage of our lives is spent plugged into an experience machine? Who is getting hurt in the process? And what opportunities for honest relationship are passing us by?

Jesus wants us to be happy—absolutely. But His call on our lives is much grander and nobler than that. As Jesus modeled, He wants us to respond with integrity to the failure of hedonism. He wants us to have tears for others. He wants those tears to unite us with a God who shed tears—a God of love and justice. He wants following that God to lead us to the sacrificial love and service of others that alone brings not only pleasure but also forgiveness, peace, purpose, and hope— the very fullness of life.

On Holy Ground
Ravi Zacharias

Prosperity, pleasure and success, may be rough of grain and common in fibre, but sorrow is the most sensitive of all created things.[1]

Those are the words of the famed pleasure seeker Oscar Wilde. In his *De Profundis,* written in prison, he expressed with profound earnestness how much sorrow had taught him. He went on to add:

Where there is sorrow there is holy ground. Some day people will realize what that means. They will know nothing of life till they do.[2]

As I reflect on those words, I first take note of the person who wrote them. A life of pain was the furthest thing from his mind when Wilde made his choices. In that sense, none of us ever really choose sorrow. But I take note of something else in his words. His claim is bold; he was not merely confessing an idea written across his worldview but one he insisted is written across the world: sorrow is holy ground, and people who do not learn to walk there know nothing of what living means. What he meant at the very least is that some of life's most sacred truths are learned in the midst of sorrow. He learned, for example, that raw, unadulterated pleasure for pleasure's sake is never fulfilling pleasure. Violation of the sacred in the pursuit of happiness is not truly a source of happiness. In fact, it kills happiness because it can run roughshod over many victims. Pleasure that profanes is pleasure that destroys.

Sorrow, on the other hand—while never pursued—comes into our lives and compels us to see our own finitude and frailty. It demands of us seriousness and tenderness if we are to live life the way it is meant to be lived. One of the most important things sorrow does is to show us what it needs and responds to. Wilde said it himself:

[Sorrow] is a wound that bleeds when any hand but that of love touches it, and even then must bleed again, though not in pain.[3]

Of all the descriptions given about Jesus, one unabashedly stands out to confront us. It is a description uttered by the prophet Isaiah, prodding mind and heart at once:

He was despised and forsaken of men,
A man of sorrows and acquainted with grief;
And like one from whom men hide their face
He was despised, and we did not esteem Him.
Surely our griefs He Himself bore,
And our sorrows He carried;
Yet we ourselves esteemed Him stricken,
Smitten of God, and afflicted.
ISAIAH 53:3-4, NASB

In our broken world, with whatever sorrows we might be experiencing, this is a description especially fitting to reflect on.

Maybe you are at a time in your life when hurt is writ large on your thoughts. Jesus is acquainted with your pain. In fact, He draws near with a hand of love. Your wound may still bleed for a while to remind you of your weakness. But He can help carry the pain in His strength. This experience could indeed be holy ground for you. It most certainly was for Him.

WEEK 6 ARTICLES

Worship on Empty
Ravi Zacharias

Years ago I read a definition of *worship* that to this day rings in clear, magnificent terms. The definition comes from the famed archbishop William Temple:

> Worship is the submission of all our nature to God. It is the quickening of conscience by His holiness; the nourishment of mind with His truth; the purifying of imagination by His beauty; the opening of the heart to His love; the surrender of will to His purpose—and all of this gathered up in adoration, the most selfless emotion of which our nature is capable.[1]

The more I have thought about that definition, the more I am convinced that if worship is practiced with integrity in the community of God's people, potentially, worship may be the most powerful evangel for this culture of ours. When people come to church, they are generally beaten down by the world of deceit, distraction, and demand. An extraction of emotional and spiritual energy brings them on empty into the community. Yet that community's task is to so prepare during the week that it is collectively the instrument of replenishment and fresh energy of soul. Even being in the presence of fellow believers in worship is meant to restore spiritual hope. We underestimate the power of a people in one mind and with one commitment. Even a prayer can so touch a hungry heart that it can rescue a sliding foot in a treacherous time.

A few years ago two or three of my colleagues and I were in a country dominated for decades by Marxism. Before we began our meetings, we were invited to a dinner hosted by some common friends, all of whom were skeptics and, for all practical purposes, atheists. The evening was full of questions, posed principally by a notable theoretical physicist in the country. Others were also present who represented different elements of power in that society. As the night wore on, we got the feeling that the questions had gone on long enough and that we were possibly going in circles.

At that point I asked if we could have a word of prayer with them, for them, and for the country before we bade them goodbye. There was a silence of consternation, an obvious hesitancy. Then one said, "Of course." We did just that; we prayed. In this large dining room of historic import to them, with all the memories of secular power plastered within those walls, the prayer brought a sobering silence that we were all in the presence of someone greater than us. When we finished, every eye was moist, and nothing was said. They hugged us and thanked us, with emotion written all over their faces. The next day when we met them, one of them said to me, "We did not go back to our rooms till it was early morning. In fact, I stayed in my hotel lobby most of the night talking further. Then I went back to my room and gave my life to Jesus Christ."

I firmly believe it was the prayer that gave them a hint of the taste of what worship is all about. Their hearts had never experienced it.

Over the years I have discovered that praying with people can sometimes do more for them than preaching to them. Prayer draws the heart away from dependence on self to leaning on the sovereign God. The burden is often lifted instantly. Prayer is only one aspect of worship but one that is greatly neglected in the face of people who would be shocked to hear what prayer sounds like when the one praying knows the heart of God. To a person in need, pat answers do not change the mind. Prayer does.[2]

Do You Believe This?
Vince Vitale

*I am the resurrection and the life. The one who believes
in me will live, even though they die; and whoever lives
by believing in me will never die. Do you believe this?*
JOHN 11:25-26

I shared these words of Jesus with the father of my oldest friend. Chris's father, Joe, was suffering from a brain tumor, and the doctors had given him only weeks to live.

When I walked in to see Joe, I did not know whether he would want to talk about his approaching death. Joe had always been strong and capable. He had a voice so deep that no matter what he was speaking about, it resounded with confidence and authority, leaving little room for vulnerability.

But as soon as Joe saw me, he said, "Hey, Vince. Good, I'm glad you're here. I told Chris I wanted to talk to you." Joe went on to tell me that although he had always been confident that God exists in some way, he was finding himself increasingly afraid about what comes next.

As we spoke, what became clear to me was that Joe's understanding of the central message of Christianity was that you should try to do more good than bad in your life and then hope that in the end your good deeds will outweigh your bad deeds. If they do, something wonderful awaits. But if they do not, you are in trouble. And as Joe reflected back over his life, he recognized that if that was the case, then he had reason to fear.

Never was I so incredibly thankful to be sitting before someone as a Christian. As an atheist, I would have had to say there is no hope beyond the grave. If I had adhered to almost any other religion, I would have had to tell Joe that he was basically right and that he had reason to fear what was next.

As a Christian, however, I was able to explain to Joe that while Christianity says God wants us to do good, our works do not make us right with God. I shared with him the message of Christianity: that what makes us right with God is not anything we do or ever could do but rather what Jesus has already done—once, in full, and for all. I explained that in Jesus we no longer need to fear judgment, because when He died, Jesus took the judgment for everything we have ever done or will ever do wrong. And we no longer need to fear suffering, shame, or even death, because Jesus has joined us in all of it and has invited us beyond it.

I explained these truths at length, and when I asked Joe if this made sense, he responded—in classic New Jersey fashion—"That's a hell of a realization." He said it again emphatically and continued, "Sixty-nine years and I never thought of that. I thought Christianity was one thing, but it was something else entirely." There was an extended pause, and then Joe said, "You know, Vince, I've spent my whole life trying to make up for my [mess]-ups, but this finally explains how I can deal with guilt." I asked Joe if he wanted to pray with me to accept this gift from God. He said he did, and with great conviction he thrust out his arm to me. We clasped hands, we wept, we prayed, and as we finished praying, he exclaimed a loud "Amen."

Joe asked me whether my wife, Jo, knew this great truth about Christ as well. I said she did, and he said, "It must be a happy life." And then, after a thoughtful pause, "Now I'm actually looking forward to what's next."

When Joe's family saw him the next day and asked how he was, for the first time in a long time he responded, "Wonderful." The transformation in him was so visible that his family immediately called me and wanted to know every word I had shared with him.

Life after death, on its own, does not bring hope. Forgiveness brings hope. Christ brings hope. And I believe, because I was there to see it, that Christ can be found with a simple, heartfelt prayer.

TIPS FOR LEADING A GROUP

Prayerfully Prepare

Prepare for each group session with prayer. Ask the Holy Spirit to work through you and the group discussion as you point to Jesus each week through God's Word.

REVIEW the weekly material and group questions ahead of time.

PRAY for each person in the group.

Minimize Distractions

Do everything in your ability to help people focus on what's most important: connecting with God, with the Bible, and with one another. Create a comfortable environment. If group members are uncomfortable, they'll be distracted and therefore not engaged in the group experience. Take into consideration seating, temperature, lighting, refreshments, surrounding noise, and general cleanliness.

At best, thoughtfulness and hospitality show guests and group members they're welcome and valued in whatever environment you choose to gather. At worst, people may never notice your effort, but they're also not distracted.

Include Others

Your goal is to foster a community in which people are welcome just as they are but encouraged to grow spiritually. Always be aware of opportunities to include and invite.

INCLUDE anyone who visits the group.

INVITE new people to join your group.

Encourage Discussion

A good small-group experience has the following characteristics.

EVERYONE PARTICIPATES. Encourage everyone to ask questions, share responses, or read aloud.

NO ONE DOMINATES—NOT EVEN THE LEADER. Be sure your time speaking as a leader takes up less than half your time together as a group. Politely guide discussion if anyone dominates.

NOBODY IS RUSHED THROUGH QUESTIONS. Don't feel that a moment of silence is a bad thing. People often need time to think about their responses to questions they've just heard or to gain courage to share what God is stirring in their hearts.

INPUT IS AFFIRMED AND FOLLOWED UP. Make sure you point out something true or helpful in a response. Don't just move on. Build community with follow-up questions, asking how other people have experienced similar things or how a truth has shaped their understanding of God and the Scripture you're studying. People are less likely to speak up if they fear that you don't actually want to hear their answers or that you're looking for only a certain answer.

GOD AND HIS WORD ARE CENTRAL. Opinions and experiences can be helpful, but God has given us the truth. Trust Scripture to be the authority and God's Spirit to work in people's lives. You can't change anyone, but God can. Continually point people to the Word and to active steps of faith.

Keep Connecting

Think of ways to connect with group members during the week. Participation during the group session is always improved when members spend time connecting with one another outside the group sessions. The more people are comfortable with one another and involved in one another's lives, the more they'll look forward to being together. When people move beyond being friendly to truly being friends who form a community, they come to each session eager to engage instead of merely attending.

Encourage group members with thoughts, commitments, or questions from the session by connecting through emails, texts, and social media.

Build deeper friendships by planning or spontaneously inviting group members to join you outside your regularly scheduled group time for meals; fun activities; and projects around your home, church, or community.

NOTES

WEEK 1

Group Session

1. Richard Dawkins, "The 'know-nothings', the 'know-alls', and the 'no contests', " *The Nullifidian,* December 1994.
2. Blaise Pascal, *The Thoughts of Blaise Pascal,* trans. C. Kegan Paul (London: George Bell, 1905), 206–7.

Personal Study 1

1. Richard Dawkins, "Is Science a Religion?" *The Humanist,* January/February 1997, http://employees.oneonta.edu/blechmjb/jbpages/m205/Richard%20 Dawkins%20Is%20Science%20A%20Religion.htm.
2. John C. Lennox, *God's Undertaker: Has Science Buried God?* (Oxford: Lion Books, 2009), 16.
3. Ibid.

Personal Study 2

1. Merriam-Webster Dictionary, s.v. "argument," accessed July 25, 2017, https:// www.merriam-webster.com/dictionary/argument.
2. Gary R. Habermas and Michael R. Licona, *The Case for the Resurrection of Jesus* (Grand Rapids, MI: Kregel, 2004), 259n24; Michael R. Licona, *The Resurrection of Jesus: A New Historiographical Approach* (Downers Grove, IL: InterVarsity, 2010), 260n25.
3. Ibid.

WEEK 2

Group Session

1. Richard Dawkins, "A Challenge to Atheists," *Free Enquiry* 22, no. 3 (2002).
2. Immanuel Kant, as quoted in *Stanford Encyclopedia of Philosophy,* s.v. "Kant's Philosophical Development," accessed July 27, 2017, https://plato.stanford.edu/ entries/kant-development.

Personal Study 1

1. Michael Ruse, *Darwinism Defended: A Guide to the Evolution Controversies* (Reading, MA: Addison-Wesley, 1982), 322, as quoted in John C. Lennox, *God's Undertaker: Has Science Buried God?* (Oxford: Lion Books, 2009), 32.
2. Lennox, *God's Undertaker*, 38.
3. Ibid., 32.
4. Ibid., 21.
5. Johannes Kepler, as quoted in Morris Kline, *Mathematics: The Loss of Certainty* (New York: Oxford University Press, 1980), 31, as quoted in Lennox, *God's Undertaker*, 21.
6. Lennox, *God's Undertaker*, 18.
7. John C. Lennox, *Seven Days That Divide the World: The Beginning According to Genesis and Science* (Grand Rapids, MI: Zondervan, 2011), 150.
8. Robert Jastrow, *God and the Astronomers* (New York: W. W. Norton, 1978), 116.

Personal Study 2

1. Paul Davies, *The Mind of God* (London: Simon and Schuster, 1992), 81, as quoted in John C. Lennox, *God's Undertaker: Has Science Buried God?* (Oxford: Lion Books, 2009), 62.
2. Albert Einstein, "Physics and Reality" (1936), reprinted in *Ideas and Opinions,* trans. Sonja Bargmann (New York: Bonanza, 1954), 292.
3. C. S. Lewis, *Mere Christianity* (New York: HarperCollins, 2001), 38.
4. Universal Declaration of Human Rights, December 10, 1948, article 1, http://www.ohchr.org/EN/UDHR/Documents/UDHR_Translations/eng.pdf.
5. Lennox, *God's Undertaker*, 40.
6. Francis J. Beckwith and Gregory Koukl, *Relativism: Feet Firmly Planted in Midair* (Grand Rapids, MI: Baker, 1998), 168.

WEEK 3

Personal Study 1

1. Ravi Zacharias, "Think Again—Deep Questions," *Just Thinking,* August 28, 2014, http://rzim.org/just-thinking/think-again-deep-questions/.

Personal Study 2

1. Abdu H. Murray, *Grand Central Question: Answering the Critical Concerns of the Major Worldviews* (Downers Grove, IL: InterVarsity, 2013), 112.
2. Clay Jones, *Why Does God Allow Evil?* (Eugene, OR: Harvest House, 2017), 80.
3. Andy Stanley, *How Good Is Good Enough?* (Sisters, OR: Multnomah Publishers, 2003), 90.
4. Augustine, *Confessions* 1:1.
5. William G. T. Shedd, *Dogmatic Theology,* 3rd ed., ed. Alan W. Gomes (Phillipsburg, NJ: Presbyterian and Reformed Publishing Company, 2003), 222.

WEEK 4

Group Study

1. Friedrich Nietzsche, *Thus Spoke Zarathustra: A Book for All and None* (Cambridge: Cambridge University Press, 2006), 75.

Personal Study 1

1. C. S. Lewis, *Mere Christianity* (San Francisco: HarperSanFrancisco, 2001), 56.
2. American Humanist Association, Humanist Manifesto III (2003), accessed August 8, 2017, https://americanhumanist.org/what-is-humanism/manifesto3/.
3. Ibid.
4. Ibid.

Personal Study 2

1. American Humanist Association, Humanist Manifesto III (2003), accessed August 8, 2017, https://americanhumanist.org/what-is-humanism/manifesto3/.
2. Richard Dawkins, *River Out of Eden: A Darwinian View of Life* (New York: HarperCollins, 1995), 132–33, as quoted in Abdu H. Murray, *Grand Central Question: Answering the Critical Concerns of the Major Worldviews* (Downers Grove, IL: InterVarsity, 2013), 70.
3. Joel Marks, "An Amoral Manifesto I," *Philosophy Now* 80 (August/September 2010): 30, as quoted in Murray, *Grand Central Question,* 76.
4. David Bentley Hart, *Atheist Delusions: The Christian Revolution and Its Fashionable Enemies* (New Haven, CT: Yale University Press, 2009), 167–68, as quoted in Murray, *Grand Central Question,* 113.

5. Dred Scott v. Sandford, 60 U.S. (19 How.) 393, 405 (1856) ("[Slaves] had no rights or privileges but such as those who held the power and the Government might choose to grant them.").

6. Os Guinness, *A Free People's Suicide: Sustainable Freedom and the American Future* (Downers Grove, IL: InterVarsity, 2012), 148.

7. American Humanist Association, Humanist Manifesto III.

8. Clay Jones, *Why Does God Allow Evil?* (Eugene, OR: Harvest House, 2017), 206.

9. Dallas Willard, *The Divine Conspiracy* (San Francisco: HarperCollins, 1998), 397, as quoted in Jones, *Why Does God Allow Evil?* 205.

WEEK 5

Group Session

1. Robert Nozick, *Anarchy, State, and Utopia* (New York: Basic Books, 1974), 42–45.

Personal Study 1

1. Mark Twain, as quoted in Clay Jones, *Why Does God Allow Evil?* (Eugene, OR: Harvest House, 2017), 165.

2. George Bernard Shaw, *A Treatise on Parents and Children* (Fairfield, IA: 1st World Library, 2004), 63, as quoted in Jones, *Why Does God Allow Evil?* 161.

3. Jack Nicholson, interview by Dotson Rader, *Parade Magazine,* December 12, 2007, http://ablogawayfromhome.blogspot.com/2007/12/interview-with-jack-nicholson-parade.html.

4. Mark Twain's letter to his wife, Olivia Clemens, July 17, 1889, as quoted in Jones, *Why Does God Allow Evil?* 100–101.

5. C. S. Lewis, *The Screwtape Letters* (New York: HarperCollins, 2001), 44.

6. Ravi Zacharias, Twitter post, February 11, 2014, 5:12 p.m., https://twitter.com/ravizacharias/status/433408300076380160?lang=en.

7. Os Guinness, *A Free People's Suicide: Sustainable Freedom and the American Future* (Downers Grove, IL: InterVarsity, 2012), 151–52.

Personal Study 2

1. C. S. Lewis, *The Problem of Pain* (New York: Macmillan, 1953), 132, as quoted in Clay Jones, *Why Does God Allow Evil?* (Eugene, OR: Harvest House, 2017), 160.

2. Westminster Shorter Catechism, Q&A #1, accessed August 17, 2017, http://www.reformed.org/documents/wsc/index.html?_top=http://www.reformed.org/documents/WSC.html.

3. Richard Swinburne, "A Theodicy of Heaven and Hell," *The Existence and Nature of God,* ed. Alfred J. Freddoso (Notre Dame: University of Notre Dame, 1983), 41, as quoted in Jones, *Why Does God Allow Evil?* 176.

WEEK 6

Personal Study 1

1. Jim Petersen and Michael Shamy, *The Insider: Bringing the Kingdom of God into Your Everyday World* (Tyndale House, 2003).
2. Portions of this content are adapted from the precourse materials of an evangelism track offered at the InterVarsity Christian Fellowship "Compelling" conference held in East Lansing, Michigan, in 2015.

Personal Study 2

1. D. A. Carson, *The Gospel According to John* (Grand Rapids, MI: Eerdmans, 1991), 215–16.
2. Ibid., 216–18.
3. Ibid., 220–21.
4. Don Everts and Doug Schaupp, *I Once Was Lost: What Postmodern Skeptics Taught Us about Their Path to Jesus* (Downers Grove, IL: InterVarsity, 2008).

Additional Resources

Week 1, Article 1

1. Adapted from *Beyond Opinion: Living the Faith We Defend,* ed. Ravi Zacharias (Thomas Nelson, 2007), 303–6.

Week 2, Article 1

1. "Is There a God?" Melbourne, Australia, July 20, 2011.
2. Stephen Hawking, *The Grand Design* (New York: Bantam, 2010), 180.
3. Quentin Smith, "The Metaphilosophy of Naturalism," *Philo* 4, no. 2 (2000).
4. Richard Dawkins, *A River Out of Eden* (New York: Perseus, 1995), 133.
5. J. R. R. Tolkien, *The Lord of the Rings* (Boston: Mariner, 2005).

Week 2, Article 2

1. Richard Dawkins, "A Challenge to Atheists," *Free Enquiry* 22, no. 3 (2002).